Enhancing Learning Through Play

A Developmental Perspective for Early Years Settings

Christine Macintyre

David Fulton Publishers Ltd
Ormond House, 26–27 Boswell Street, London WC1N 3JZ

www.fultonpublishers.co.uk

First published in Great Britain by David Fulton Publishers 2001

Note: The right of Christine Macintyre to be identified as the author of this work has been asserted by her in accordance with the Copyright, Designs and Patents Act 1988.

British Library Cataloguing in Publication Data
A catalogue record for this book is available from the British Library

ISBN 1–85346–761–8

Typeset by Textype Typesetters, Cambridge
Printed in Great Britain by The Cromwell Press Ltd, Trowbridge, Wilts.

Contents

Acknowledgements

There are many children and adults who have contributed to this book and my thanks go to them all. It is a privilege to be allowed to come into early years settings and enjoy the children who are happy and hard at work as they play. The teachers, nursery nurses and classroom assistants are unfailingly generous in sharing their ideas, their hopes and their worries, and indeed it was their concern that the intrinsic learning within play was not being appreciated by curriculum planners, and that a more formal curriculum might be imposed, that prompted this book. Thank you too to the parents who gave me permission to take the photographs of their enchanting children. They help to keep the text lively and show that research happens in the real world.

I hope that the photographs will show the children's enthusiasm for the range of activities which all come under the umbrella term 'play', and that the text will demonstrate the complex concerns which guide the teachers' planning. How *do* they plan when children have so many different interests and different abilities? It is not an easy thing to do. All of the adults observe the children carefully to find their level of coping in all aspects of their development and through discussion and debate and lots of experience, they build learning opportunities so that each child's profile of abilities may be enhanced. They listen carefully to the parents so that their wishes and concerns are part of the learning scenario too. In this way they provide meaningful and appropriate learning with the child, the important one, at the centre of it all.

Foreword

A book which has at its heart not merely a justification of play, but an emphatic demand that it be regarded as an essential vehicle for early learning, could not be more topical, coming as it does in the aftermath of the publication of the Foundation Stage documentation. It is within the pages of the latter that practitioners are urged to respond to the need for planned opportunities for play within the curriculum. Nothing new there, many might say. However, practitioners working in all areas of early learning and child care have seen the term 'play' used to describe a whole raft of activities from higher-order learning to occupation of the most unfulfilling kind. In this book, Dr Macintyre involves the reader in the importance of education and the contribution of play to successfully motivating learners. In so doing, she raises the often perplexing issue of the role of the adult as observer, supporter and sometime director of that play. This, in itself, provides practitioners with valuable guidance and support and encourages them to become more confident in allowing children to manage their own play, and in consequence to have a greater control over their own learning. This in turn, forces practitioners to evaluate their contribution to play rather than seeing their input as always impacting positively on the outcome.

The text also focuses on the subject of child development and in so doing provides student teachers and other professionals with a valuable source of reference. In acknowledging the fact that a pre-requisite of being able to teach a child is the need to know that child in an holistic way, the author is ensuring that the study of child development is accorded a positive and indeed essential status.

This book is both informative and user-friendly and its organisation allows readers to 'dip' in and out of sections according to their needs. Although it will be regarded as a valuable source of reference for students, it is a highly readable text for all early years practitioners involved in both education and child care and will provide them with an ally, should they require one, in ensuring the rightful place of play within an effective early years curriculum.

Jenny Clement, Early Years Advisor
January 2001

Introduction

Everyone wants children to be healthy and happy and to make the most of the opportunities that come their way. In the early years, families, teachers, nursery nurses and possibly other carers work together to achieve these hugely important goals. But how is it to happen? How are children, with their different personalities, aptitudes and interests to be guided so that they are happy and fulfilled? What do all these people who wish to help need to know?

This book is written to answer these sorts of questions. It does so by explaining the different aspects of child development and highlighting what most children can do at different ages and stages in their lives. This is so assessments and comparisons against these norms can be made and learning activities can be designed to match and extend what the children can do. Strategies to help children whose development is 'extraordinary' in any way are also included.

Such assessment is best done when the children are learning naturally, without stress, i.e. when they are at play. For young children play is the same as work and adults can build on this to structure play opportunities and support children as they learn. But before being able to do this in any meaningful way, they have to know the developmental trends which happen for all children. Then they can be sure that both the nature of the support and its timing are the most helpful and appropriate.

But why through play? Surely children go to school to learn 'other things'? Surely they have had plenty of time to play at home? The thing is that play in play group and nursery has its own set of demands and learning possibilities. Children learn to cooperate with others, and learn what others can do. They develop language skills; they interact with children who have been brought up differently from themselves and so learn to appreciate each other and respect the customs and perspectives which affect different childhoods. They learn the routine of school

and come to understand the rules of this new community. All of this helps them develop the planning and organisational skills which underpin so much of learning. And all of this happens through play.

This is why play is such a critically important part of an early years' curriculum. Teachers set up learning opportunities based on the children's interests, often in the form of play corners. One of the aims of this book is to show the learning which can be incorporated into this kind of plan, for although the children might be seen to be 'just playing', all the time they are learning, just as fast as they can.

But not all children like playing. Some find it impossible to play. Why should this be? Again a developmental framework provides some of the answers. Dividing this complex study into different aspects, i.e. intellectual development, perceptual-motor development, social and emotional development, ensures that all the various and varying intricacies of how each child develops can be explained. Growing and learning is a journey each child must take. Easing the path and trying to ensure that each child travels smoothly, is surely a worthwhile thing to do.

Play within a more formal curriculum

The new millennium heralds an era of early intervention in literacy and mathematics, testing for children and appraisal for teachers. Given the pressure of meeting targets and obtaining favourable results, is there a danger that in school, children will have less time and opportunity to play? And if television and computer games at home co-exist with 'safe' leisure activities where the children once more practise and perfect specific skills, will there be still less time for child-led activities where the children make choices, develop their imaginations and play their own games? What are the implications? Will the children be harried and hurried to the detriment of a balanced development? Will they be stressed? Might children even lose the ability to play?

Of course it is very important that all children achieve a range of key competences, or 'coping skills', and those who set tests and targets hope that the directed teaching which results will enable more children to be more competent more quickly, i.e. that they will achieve the prescribed goals faster. The pressure of so doing, however, means that there is likely to be less time for either free or structured play, fewer opportunities for children to decide what they would like to do and to determine their own pace of learning. To achieve the targets the children must conform to an 'outside' notion of what education in school is for, and to someone else's idea of what they should learn. They must, in following that agenda, confront someone else's problems rather than setting and solving their own.

Possibly, decisions about providing adequate time for play in the curriculum depend on the prevailing beliefs about the purpose of young children's learning. Is education in the nursery and infant classrooms primarily a time to learn a set of prescribed skills? Or is is a time to learn to be confident and self-reliant or expressive and imaginative? Are these mutually exclusive goals or is a 'good education' a balance of the two, i.e. being given enough guidance to attain necessary skills and understandings yet enough freedom to make choices? Pollard (1996) claims that 'the key issue is the contrast between an understanding of education as the inculcation of established knowledge versus its definition as a process of helping learners to construct their own insights and understandings.'

This is a very difficult dilemma but it is a critically important one, for the contrast highlights the distinction between two different emphases that and inform curriculum planning.

The first is primarily concerned with children learning what we know, or at least the skills and competences which, again in our opinion, will enable them to be employed and 'do well' in a competitive world. The second is less adamant and more trusting. Based on understandings about children's development, it provides the resources and opportunities to match their developing competences, thus helping children learn, but it does not to the same extent, specify the content or the outcome. It believes that very young children know intuitively what they need to do and so they base their learning on their own motivation and interests. Teachers observe children carefully and on the basis of observing what the children are doing and assessing that through their knowledge of the learning plan and their understanding of developmental norms, they support and extend the children's learning in the most helpful and appropriate way.

Children spend many years in school and so educators must have a clear picture of what they are for. New ways must be better ways. Successful tried and tested ways must not be jettisoned without a clear rationale for so doing and a convincing argument about what is to take their place. Surely, as children mature they wish to have different methods of teaching, not just more of the same? The early years provide a wonderful opportunity for children to be happy and fulfilled. Everything must be done to remove the word 'boring' from their evaluation of their time in school.

Another recent development is the entry of more three-year-olds into early education with, in some regions, priority being given to those from less advantaged backgrounds in the hope that immersion in nurseries will compensate for their restricted or unhelpful lifestyle. While this sounds ideal, the children must have the level of development to allow them to benefit, the new learning must not be too far removed from the old or it will be confusing, and above all the 'head start' must last beyond the time when rote learning can give the impression of meaningful learning. In the past some head start programmes, set up with the best of intentions and hailed to have benefited underprivileged children, have not had lasting results. While immediate improvement was noted, it was not sustained and children without the intervention soon caught up. This raised questions about the readiness of the studied group to absorb more formal learning and, in my view, made a strong case for letting children learn through free and structured play.

Three-year-old entry to nurseries poses another set of concerns for teachers and nursery nurses and challenges the curriculum in terms of differentiating learning to encompass these young children's needs. What kinds of things will they need to know? What will they be able to do? How will they fit in with the four- and five-year-olds? Will they not need even more time to play? Intervention to 'teach them how' would need to be carefully planned and justified to allay the fears of researchers such as Cohen (1987) who, contemplating the process of children's maturation and learning and being afraid that being asked to do too much too soon was counter-productive, grimly asked 'Are there social engineers on the swings?'

In the light of the ongoing debate about the content of the curriculum and the optimum mode of delivering it, about the effect of children's changing recreational pursuits on children's health and socialisation as well as their education, it is timely to reconsider and re-evaluate the contribution that play in its many forms can make to the development of young children. This would allow teachers to justify its inclusion as an important part of the curriculum and, when appropriate, to have the courage to give the children time and space to play – secure in the knowledge that they are engaged in meaningful learning – meaningful, that is to curriculum developers and, even more importantly, to the children themselves. Being able to articulate this justification would allow those who support the inclusion of play to spell out what it is that children are learning and possibly persuade those who want young children to do 'other things' that play is real learning, particularly suited to the children's experience and stage of development, and therefore without stress.

The value of play as an epistemic (learning), or ludic (practising), cathartic (letting off steam and reducing stress), or therapeutic (releasing fears through acting them out) activity, has been endorsed by teachers, psychoanalysts and psychologists, by parents and by the children themselves who almost universally love playing. Why then should other activities push aside the time they have for play? Perhaps the answer to this question is linked to the earlier one, i.e. what is education in school for? If it is primarily to pass tests and to get ready for the next phase of exams, then the most efficient way to do this may be to engage in direct teaching episodes and simply to tell the children what they need to know. In this scenario, the learning outcomes can be prescribed in advance and the children's achievements can be readily 'measured' against pre-set criteria. As a result, teachers can be confident that at least some of the children are learning the same things and to the same standard.

Alternatively, if education is about enabling children to confront new, stimulating challenges, confident that they can try appropriate and innovative ways of meeting them, then a different kind of learning experience needs to be encountered. A different set of criteria built on imagination, perception and the ability to sustain involvement until a solution is found, needs to be conceptualised. The outcomes will be less tangible and less easily measured, but are they then less important? Certainly they will not be met through any approach which sees letting children play as an easier option. Adopting an unconsidered laissez-faire approach which just lets the children flounder without guidance and stimulation is not part of this equation. Guiding play and building activities based on 'where the children are at' and having the perception and observation skills to guide them into more complex but appropriate ways of learning while letting them retain control is a very difficult thing to do. It is much easier to fill them up with things, possibly readily measured things, that they 'should' know.

Perhaps parents and teachers will decide that both kinds of learning experiences must be included in an early years' curriculum. Maybe then children can have the best of both worlds. To achieve this, educators must not allow the technocratic aspects of education to push out the imaginative ones where children can retain some decision-making powers and be the prime movers in their own education. If this does happen, perhaps as Wordsworth feared, 'Shades of the prison house will begin to close upon the growing boy.'

Aware of this fear, this book tries to justify a curriculum which houses lots of play. Based on a developmental framework, i.e. looking at the four aspects of development, it shows how understanding development is an essential part of developing stimulating and motivating learning activities which at all times start with the child. Also considered are 'other' complex issues which confront many children and often leave parents and teachers wondering how best to cope, e.g. 'not wanting to stay at nursery', 'having imaginary friends', 'being clumsy' and 'helping children who find it difficult to play'. The book also considers the thorny issue of intervention, aware of Cohen's (1987) cry, 'How can we, long out of practice oldies, tell children how to play?' and Roberts' (1995) claim that, 'Supportive interactions are crucial for the development of young children.'

Above all it is written to encourage teachers to believe that young children, engrossed in their own experiences, can be trusted to keep playing and keep learning, just sometimes in spite of what others try to do!

CHAPTER 1

Play and learning

Most young children love to play and love to learn although the things they like to play at, and indeed the things they like to learn, change as they mature. Some informal research carried out by student teachers at Edinburgh University had a surprising outcome. It found that children at primary school nominated 'the best times of the day' as 'time to play' and 'time to go home'! If this is generally the case, then, as children do spend many hours in school, we must surely try to discover why these adult-free times are the children's 'best choices'. The children explained that they 'really preferred play to work', although they were less able to say what the difference was!

One way for adults to pinpoint the difference and thereby identify the characteristics of each would be to focus on one activity such as reading a book and tease out what it is that makes one scenario 'play' and another very similar one 'work' (see Table 1.1).

Table 1.1 Reading a book

	Play	**Work**
Selecting a book	Chosen by the reader	Imposed on the reader
Language	The reader chooses the level of difficulty, readily understands the meaning	May be too difficult, e.g. with specialist terminology
Purpose	Enjoyment, relaxation To deepen interest in the chosen topic	Extend knowledge Deepen understanding
Pace	Chosen by the reader	Must meet deadlines set elsewhere
Additional action	None. Can skim over text or miss parts	Memorising; analysing; criticising; linking theory to practice; evaluating
Tension	Can abandon book if unfinished	Must finish the set task and try to do it well

From my attempt to do this, you can see that 'freedom' and 'choice,' i.e. to continue reading or not to trouble, are key characteristics of play. Important too are 'outside' expectations and the pressure which results from their fulfilment. In play there is no end product, no time pressure and so there is no fear of failure. Moreover, because the activity is chosen by the players themselves, one can assume that it is pleasing to them; it is fun.

Play then:

- is enjoyable, freely chosen by the player,
- can be abandoned without blame,
- has no preconceived outcome; the agenda can develop as play goes on,
- gives pleasure and often counteracts stress,
- develops skills which are important in non-play, i.e. work situations.

This sounds ideal. Is play then always fun? Do children and adults always prefer to play? Of course not. Think of the children left out of playground games and those who find it very difficult to follow the rules of someone else's game. For them, playing is an ordeal much harder perhaps than the activities they think of as work. Children 'not allowed to play' are unhappy children – their rejection is likely to be public and humiliating. Classroom inadequacies can be hidden away and discussed later or they can be derided, 'Who wants to do that anyway?' but 'not getting to play' is a heartrending state of affairs which impacts cruelly on the self-esteem. Adult pleas to 'let him join in' have usually only temporary success, if they work at all. And what of adults who feel compelled to play despite their dread of small-talk at the party or that never ending round of golf? For social reasons or health reasons or promotion reasons they feel they must conform and do the done thing, i.e. fulfil other peoples' expectations. And as the freedom element has been taken away, the fun and enjoyment disappear too.

As we strive to understand more about play, it could be helpful to consider the different reasons people give for playing. As you read them, think of whether they could best be applied to adults or children or equally to both. Perhaps you would like to analyse your own reasons for playing in this kind of way?

- Fun reasons – for enjoyment,
- skill reasons – to improve some aspect of performance,
- social reasons – to make or meet friends, the activity itself being less important,
- fitness reasons – to maintain or increase health,
- challenging reasons – taking risks; seeking thrills,
- vertigo reasons – activities which involve almost losing control, e.g. hang gliding,
- cathartic reasons – seeking release from pressures elsewhere.

The list above shows very different reasons for playing and probably they could apply to both adults and children. Understanding the reason why is important for those who wish to intervene – to help the players do it better perhaps. It is not difficult to see why tensions arise if a player who has come to play badminton primarily to meet friends and have a pleasant social round is confronted by someone who wishes to advise on technique. And while the adult can explain or walk away, children can be left bemused or confused or resentful that their play has been spoiled. It is important that both parties understand the purpose or reason for doing!

But while these characteristics of play sound enticing and the reasons for doing it illuminating, there is really only one reason, i.e. the developing skill reason, that overtly suggests that learning is part of play. And of course the critical questions over time have always been: 'Do children learn as they play? And if they do, what do they learn? And if they don't, what is it that they do?'

To answer these questions, let's remember Isaacs' (1933) description of play – one which has endured over time. She claimed that, 'Play is a child's life and the means by which he comes to understand the world he lives in.'

She considered that play was the crucial component in children's development. In fact she found that young children's work and play was (to them) the same thing! She urged everyone concerned with young children to recognise and value the different kinds of understandings which developed through play. What did she envisage? Well, in the earliest days, that understanding might be learning how to build relationships and finding what kind of cries brought food or comfort or instant attention. Sometime later, role play at home or at school could help children assimilate the mores of their particular culture, for in play children can safely enact the things they have seen around them. Practising being more grown up than they really are, usually meets with praise and support. Perhaps this is why Vygotsky (1978) claims that in play, 'a child is always above his average age . . . in play it is as if a child is trying to jump above the level of his usual behaviour.'

And if children can try things with no fear of failure they are more likely to stretch out and tackle things they might otherwise avoid. Whether these activities are seen as primarily practice or primarily learning may well depend on how they are approved by the important others in the child's life, how well the implicit learning in the activity is recognised and understood and indeed on the pace at which new skills or understandings are mastered. Observing and assessing the implicit learning in play is not an easy thing to do. The results and, therefore, the value given to the activity may well depend on the understanding and observation skills of the observers! Subtle forms of learning may be missed.

Example
One early learning/play activity is 'peek-a-boo'. Observed at a superficial level, the game could be seen as just a lighthearted bit of fun. Closer examination, however, reveals that turn-taking, i.e. waiting and acting and reacting, is important social learning; indeed this kind of game, one where reciprocity is a 'rule', is thought to be vitally important in emerging communication.

Wells (1986) explains that language itself develops only because children strive for a means to be understood. 'What urges young children into speech' he claims, 'is their desire to communicate their intentions more precisely.' Certainly these researchers, i.e. Isaacs, Vygotsky and Wells, are sure that children are learning as they play.

If this truly happens, if children, through playing learn successfully on their own, why are adults so anxious to intervene? Why must the children learn more formal 'teaching things' earlier and earlier? Does the new generation have more things to learn? Will they run out of time? Is that why the pressure is on? Perhaps adults forget how much time new learning takes and how necessary hands-on experience is, for 'doing' is a purposeful way of learning (Lally 1991). Listening to instructions is a difficult mode for very young children who may lack concentration skills or the kind of experiences which can help their learning.

Or perhaps we cannot be sure that this spontaneous learning will happen for all children? We all know children who prefer to repeat the same activity over and over again with no obvious increase in understanding or skill or any seeming motivation to change. Instead of imposing other things upon them, should we be pausing and asking why? Could repetition be giving confidence and security in a world where things are changing too fast? If so, then repetition is contributing to the development of the self as an independent being. These children certainly aren't standing still. Perhaps we should all take more time to stand and contemplate a little more. Perhaps our actions might be more thoughtful, even more effective for that?

Let's divide play activities under the headings 'play as learning' and 'play as practice' now and see what differences emerge (Figure 1.1).

It is interesting to realise that the same activities can fit into either category depending on the intention, the attitude and aptitude of the player. A child cutting paper with scissors for the first time is learning manipulative skills and something about the properties of paper, e.g. that firm paper cuts more easily with safety scissors. This activity would go into column 1, 'play as learning'. The child might then practise for some time just for the sake of it, until such time as the novelty wore off and a new challenge came in sight. This spell would go into column 2, 'play as practice.' However when different materials were available for cutting, or when the children cut out different shapes or when the children had to judge which materials were the most suitable for a particular purpose, i.e. when there was a new problem, then the activity would swing back into column 1, 'play as learning'. Suffice to say that in most activities there are elements of new learning which need to be practised if a skilled performance is to be achieved. Most children will practise until they can achieve a level of skill which pleases them and then, when they are ready, they move on. Playground games with balls and skipping ropes are examples of this. Suddenly the games appear and suddenly they go. No adult decrees when!

And so there are different perspectives on children's play. Some see play as the vehicle for learning while others claim that in play any new learning is incidental and that play is mainly a time for practice. Certainly Meadows and Cashdan (1998) consider that childrens' play, 'is often brief and desultory, not amounting to anything fruitful.' Perhaps then is the time to offer help.

Of course as children mature, their play changes and links between different types of play and different chronological ages have been claimed. In Figure 1.1, the subheadings list these and they are now explained in greater detail.

Play as Learning	Play as Practice
Constructive Play Making models or building with some thought given to planning or purpose or design	*Sensori-motor Play* Exploring objects, i.e. feeling and tasting them; building a tower, pouring water from one jug to another; drawing the same picture
Explorative Play Finding the properties of new objects and discovering what they can do	*Symbolic Play* Using objects to represent live things (e.g. a yo-yo as a dog on a lead) or incomplete objects (e.g. using an empty cup to feed a doll)
Problem Solving Completing jigsaws and other puzzles; cutting and glueing to make a collage; choosing appropriate materials	*Fantasy and Sociodramatic Play* Role playing e.g. being a spaceman or a nurse; using an object to represent something else, e.g. a cardboard box as a spaceship
Games with Rules Participating with increasing understanding of turn-taking; using a dice; knowing how to move and when to move	*Rough and Tumble Play* Pretend fighting; falling over obstacles; physically demanding play
Play on Apparatus Climbing more skilfully; jumping to land safely	*Motor Skill Play* Throwing a ball into the air and catching it (without varying the distance or speed); cutting paper (to practise using scissors)
Language Play Building rhythms and rhymes; word play	

More complex games with rules
Competitive play involving techniques and tactics, anticipation of an opponent's play and taking appropriate action

Figure 1.1 Play as learning and play as practice

Different kinds of play

As babies become toddlers and toddlers children, they gain competence in all aspects of their development (intellectual, social, emotional and perceptual-motor). These developing capacities together with their various and varied experiences of the environment allow them to increase the number of things they can do. And so it is with play. And as they grow, children play at different things. Researchers who have studied these differences (Piaget and Inhelder 1969; Rubin *et al.* 1983) have found that free play progresses in a pre-determined way. Although it could be misleading to call these differences 'stages', as the behaviours mingle and mix rather than change abruptly, there are qualitative differences in the types of play which children exhibit as they grow older and these are now described.

Sensori-motor play

At around four months, children play with their hands, their first toy. They are fascinated by the patterns they make and gradually realise two things. The first is that these hands belong to them and they have control over them, the second is that they can be used to hit, then grasp objects which are out there in space. These early movement patterns are very important in developing coordination and efficient movement. As babies reach out to grasp they are making movement decisions – spatial ones: how far do I reach? and in what direction?; timing ones: when do I open my hand to grasp? when do I let go? how fast do I need to move? and body boundary ones: where do I end and where does the toy begin? The children are developing coordination through these early movements which when practised will become habitual and automatic. Through all of this playful activity, which can be hard work, the children are building 'practical intelligence', i.e. a store of skills which will form the basis of a repertoire of many movements.

Slightly later the baby is testing the properties of objects by sucking them (as the mouth is very sensitive and conveys messages of hardness or softness or different tastes) and needs supervision to ensure small objects are not swallowed. Taste discrimination precedes that of object size! In all of this exploratory play, the baby, without any tutoring, is learning what objects can do and learning to handle them with increasing dexterity. Later still, at nine months or so, the ability to crawl opens up a new play vista. Toys can be retrieved, taken to another place or moved along the floor. Cupboards formerly out of range can be reached and emptied – the contents providing lots of problem-solving activities – although the problem of fitting them back into place is usually abandoned!

Constructive play

By 18 months children enjoy building with bricks and knocking the edifice down. They replace the bricks with increasing dexterity, using the fingers and thumb, i.e. a pincer grip to grasp rather than the whole hand which makes letting go difficult.

They enjoy repetitive play and anticipating the same surprise as in peek-a-boo games. They begin to show interest in simple puzzles such as inset boards or five-piece jigsaws and they will applaud any that are completed. At two years plus, they will make snakes with play-dough. At this stage, toys are used for their real purpose, a spoon is a spoon!

Symbolic play

Between two and three years, children use one object to represent another, i.e. one as a symbol of another. Their developing imaginations allow them to pretend, e.g. that a wooden brick is a car and they will drive the brick along the pretend road with accompanying realistic noises. At this stage children stay immersed in their games for a longer spell because they have the physical ability to move around and many more ideas about what different objects do. Just as they can now pretend or imagine one thing is something else, they also begin to pretend that they themselves are other people – this is the start of role play.

At age two, children also begin to play 'in parallel' rather than in the solitary way they did earlier. This means that they will play alongside other children making occasional contact with them, e.g. briefly showing interest in what they are doing or moving towards them to show their own play. These communications gradually lengthen and lead to children playing together, perhaps engaging in cooperative role play. This appears earlier in siblings who share the same stories and other experiences.

Sociodramatic play

The three- and four-year-old children, who now play together rather than alone, enact all the roles they see around them and demonstrate detailed understanding of their perceptions of mummy, daddy and baby, doctor, nurse and patient and even characters in their favourite stories. Often a great deal of time can be taken up in allocating and rejecting parts to the detriment of the real game ever beginning at all! The smallest children are very often given the 'baddie' parts because they are the ones who do not fully understand the character of the role they have to play – or it may be the only way they are allowed to join in – or they may not have the language it takes to refuse! At this age the dominant players in a group of children are emerging. It is best if the same ones do not lead all of the time.

This is the time when many children have imaginary companions and give them a special role as friend or dog or whatever. For a time these friends are very real to the children and seem to support them just as a pet does. Adults can feel strange having to search for lost imaginary friends or having to set a place for them at table, but they can be reassured that this phase will pass for it is a normal part of the development of pretence (Taylor *et al.* Carlsen 1993). An imaginary friend, who of course always agrees and who makes no demands, can help the child, providing a secure base, almost a retreat, so that the worries of the day can be shared. The 'friend' can also make comments that the child is wary of putting forward, and when the suggestion misfires, take the blame!

Example

My own daughter had an imaginary best friend, 'Jane'. She went everywhere – we had to be careful not to sit on her in the car and she had her own set of eating likes and dislikes which were listed regularly! Moreover, she was usually blamed for any mishap, 'Must've been Jane', and sometimes she was used as a shelter, 'Jane says she's not going to do that . . .' or 'Jane's a silly girl to want the light on, but she does.' One day a scream from the back of the car nearly had us in the ditch. The scream was because 'Jane has been left in Dindal' (Dingwall, a holiday place 200 miles distant). The fact that we couldn't return to collect her was met by howls and heartbreaking sobs until we had the brainwave to say we'd pick her up at the airport! Jane lasted for months but suddenly we realised she had disappeared. Maybe the child had grown confident enough to cope on her own?

Any kind of role-playing can help develop altruism, i.e. caring for someone else at some cost to yourself, as children, taking the part of a parent or a nurse, begin to appreciate the demands of that role. In this way they may become less self-centred and see the world from the viewpoint of another person – they move from being egocentric to becoming sociocentric. This is important social learning in helping them move into a wider society.

An important change happens when five- and six-year-olds become able to plan ahead. Now they can indicate what game will be played and visualise a sequence of events even to deciding how the game will end. Tears and battles can occur if not all of the players understand the proposed sequences or agree with them. Indeed the planners may expect others to share their understanding without ever having explained what the game was about at all! For children who cannot empathise and understand that others may have different views, playing can be confusing and bewildering.

Games with rules

Very often the rules of games are not explained to novice players, they are learned by playing the game. Very early games have simple rules – the adult in the peek-a-boo game will demonstrate carefully what is to happen and play patiently till the babies understand. As the games become more complex, the first-time player can have a difficult time observing and understanding the rules. In a game of 'I spy with my little eye', a four-year-old had a wonderful time disclaiming the efforts of her older friends who guessed everything imaginable for the letter 'W'. When they eventually gave in and asked for the solution, the child looked blank – no one had explained that she had to have identified an object beginning with 'W' herself. Did anyone ever explain that to you?

Interestingly, as the spontaneous games of the early years disappear and are replaced by 'recognised' games, e.g. rounders, card games or board games, the rules are made explicit on paper, although young children often adapt the game, e.g. snakes and ladders or Monopoly to suit their own level of understanding. Playing is much more complex and winning emerges as a new goal. Now children must learn the rules and practise the moves if they are to get better at playing.

And so there are many kinds of play differing in the resources and the amount of structure provided by adults. As a result children have variety and stimulation and so are enabled to learn many things. In structuring play activities and by carefully supporting children, adults hope that the benefits of play can be retained as more formal learning is introduced. Through different kinds of play, children can in a safe environment.

Experiment to find:

- how things work,
- the effect altering one thing has on another, e.g. what happens to ice in warm water,
- the different properties of materials, e.g. wet and dry sand, and how these affect building,
- how different materials make different sounds,
- what kind of planning is necessary to accomplish a task.

Understand:

- the responsibilities different people have, e.g. fireman, nurse, parents, and how they carry out their jobs,
- how different children react to being involved in a game, e.g. one child might smack a doll as punishment, another could be horrified by this response,
- that different people have different perceptions/ ideas/ evaluations.

Imagine:

- scenes they have not experienced, e.g. meeting a friendly alien and travelling to his land,
- how stories could end, what different outcomes might be,

- how others feel in their role, e.g. dancers on a stage or television.

Create:

- models, e.g. of castles in the wet sand,
- collages, e.g. using materials or sticky paper to make a scene,
- gifts for home, using threading or weaving or gluing.

Act out:

- their own worries in a sheltered environment, e.g. going into hospital or sharing their toys with a new baby.

To derive full benefit from all these possibilities, adults need to provide the time, the resources and sometimes the ideas to start the children off or help them continue. In this way their learning can be extended in a myriad of ways and all through play.

The first question, 'What is play?' has been considered in general terms and the second, 'What is learning?' now takes the stage.

What is learning?

It goes without saying that learning has occurred when children know something new or are able to do something that was not possible before. But what is involved? And could the learning process be eased? Claxton (1990) claims that, 'Learning always involves a modification of what you already believe or know. Right from the moment we are born, all learning involves the proliferation and differentiation of what we knew the moment before.'

And so, although children may not be aware of reflecting, new learning occurs more easily if it is built on these previous understandings and/or experiences. This usually means that the gap between the old and the new is small and for the children, manageable. Following Piaget's (1977) advice, it is best to have a balance of new learning and familiar activities so that the children can be successful and, through gaining confidence, eager to learn more.

Claxton's (1990) claim highlights the importance of the many and varied learning experiences the children have and have had outside school, and new learning can readily be built on these. This is why the recognition of parents as early and continuing educators is so important. Munn (1994) explains that it is the high degree of prior knowledge which parents have of their children's aptitudes and experiences which facilitates their children's learning. By talking through shared outings, selecting stories which their children enjoy and just through knowing the people and the pets the children know, shared meaning or 'intersubjectivity' can be readily established. Rogoff (1990) also acknowledges the value of parental input. She tells how 'parents routinely adjust their interaction and structure children's environments in ways consistent with providing support for learning.'

How do they do this? The strategies which parents most successfully use are:

- listening carefully to what the child has to say
- trying hard to understand the child's meaning
- following the child's agenda, and
- pitching their own intervention just beyond their child's usual level of competence.

As a result they provide a 'contingent response to their child's curiosity' (Wells 1986). In nurseries and schools teachers and nursery nurses aim to do this too. However they sometimes lack access to enough 'prior understanding' for each individual child. And although they actively seek out opportunities to talk with individual children, they are usually coping with a group who may have very different home backgrounds and varied interests. This makes planning appropriate learning scenarios very difficult.

Not knowing about the children can also make conversations superficial and meaningless. Often arid questions, i.e. those which only require a one-word answer, result, e.g. 'What colour are your shoes?', and so learning possibilities are lost. Aware of this, teachers try to familiarise themselves with the children's background using strategies like talking with the parents at every opportunity, or asking the children to bring in a photo of themselves at home so that they might prepare some meaningful interaction. Of course when this happens, the children then expect the teachers to know the cat's name, who lives next door, and can be incredulous, even scornful, when those details aren't known. But a move to decentre and understand the children's background so that 'conversations' can be meaningfully shared is an important step towards being able to extend the children's learning, perhaps by introducing new words and new concepts to their existing vocabulary, or choosing stories or designing activities which are based on their interests.

Talking of very early learning experiences raises another question, i.e.

When do children begin to learn?

The only answer is 'right from the start,' in fact Trevarthen (1993) finds that,

'One of the difficulties in working with newborns is that they have minds of their own!'

Over the years there have been many debates about the onset of learning and these have influenced childrearing practices. Feeding at strictly four-hourly intervals so that a routine would be established was replaced by feeding on demand. While this may seem a trivial example it shows a change in willingness to acknowledge that babies know what is best, at least for themselves! Babies' clothes have changed from pastel shades to bright colours following research which identified babies' preferences; now teddies and other soft toys are replaced by mobiles and musical toys which need thought and concentration to make them work. Stimulation, problem solving and practice are now key words, even for the very young.

Piaget placed this kind of action and self-directed problem solving at the heart of learning and development. He found that even in the cot, children with problems to solve, e.g. how do I reach out to pull the string to start the music?, were not moving aimlessly but with a purpose and this helped them develop movement patterns or schema (in the above case, reaching and grasping), which could transfer to other tasks or coping skills. Increasing dexterity could then lead to more complex movements being tried. The important thing was that the action and decision making was left for the children – the joy of discovery and success was theirs. The children also decided how long they wished to practise before abandoning one skill and progressing to the next.

In the introduction to the video *Play for Tomorrow*, Trevarthen (1993) made some significant, even startling claims. These were that:

- the years between birth and five are marked by significant change,
- 50% of intellectual development happens in the first five years,
- the brain of every child in every culture goes through certain crucial developmental stages,
- there are certain times when the brain craves certain kinds of stimuli, and so
- children require the right experiences at the right times.

And as Trevarthen used imaging equipment to discern and monitor activity within the child's brain and found that this increased markedly when new challenges were tackled, he was able to be sure that 'young children are thirsting for new knowledge.' Given this eagerness to learn, all who are involved with young children will be anxious to know what these 'right experiences' and 'right times' are.

This important link between understanding children's development and realising the implications for teaching is apparent in Trevarthen's statements. These indicate the responsibility teachers have for identifying the stage of development of each child and thereafter preparing activities to extend their learning. And through stressing the timing of learning (Piaget called these times 'critical periods'), Trevarthen is suggesting that learning may be more difficult if particularly receptive times are missed. Think of the difficulty many adults have in learning a second language, learning to use a computer, even learning to ski. And yet children do these things with ease. Perhaps the phrase 'You can't teach an old dog new tricks,' originated here! The surprise may be that those critical times come so early. Curriculum planners must be aware of the possible timing of these so that the most appropriate pace and content of teaching can be planned. It is also important that they do not underestimate the abilities young children possess.

Claxton (1990) also recognised that children needed to learn things that could not be based on their previous knowledge base. How was this to come about? He claimed that, 'if new learning is not engaged with current understanding, it will be ignored, or if it must be retained then certain special skills will be called upon.'

These special skills include concentrating, memorising and learning a range of problem-solving strategies.

Concentrating

A very important aid to learning is being able to concentrate. This influences how readily children learn and how much they learn. Even in the earliest years there is a marked difference in the way children use this learning strategy. Some nursery

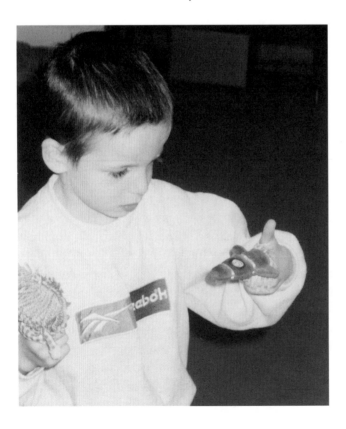

children concentrate for an inordinate amount of time showing grit and perseverance until a problem is resolved. Sometimes they even ask for more time to spend on one activity. Interestingly, this application seems to be pervasive – it is not confined to one particular kind of activity. This means that the ability to concentrate is within the child rather than something which fluctuates depending on the activity on offer. Teachers usually claim that concentration is a good indicator of potential and applaud this kind of approach. Children who concentrate are therefore likely to have positive reinforcement to continue. On the other hand many children are easily distracted from the task at hand. Parents and teachers are constantly heard complaining about 'lack of ability to concentrate'. Children who can't concentrate tend to flit from one activity to another and show little evidence of learning. Their attention span is impulsive and brief. Why should this be?

Wood (1992) found that many young children just have not developed the capacity for retaining involvement and he surmised that this was due to their lack of organisational ability – the children could neither organise the materials they required for successful completion of the task nor visualise the end product. If this is so, it can be seen why tasks are abandoned. The best kind of help could be discussing the planning and resources and helping the children decide on the sequence of events which will enable them to complete a task. Asking the children to sit and concentrate is self-defeating if the underlying abilities are not developed. They need to be shown how to organise and plan their work. There is a subtle but important distinction between helping children complete the end product, be it a painting, a model or a puzzle, and helping them with the process, i.e. the organisation – what preparation is needed, what action comes when. As more becomes known about conditions such as dyspraxia, the importance of helping children plan what they wish to do rather than help them complete the end product becomes more and more significant (Macintyre 2000).

Memorising

A second ability is memorising, with or without really understanding the meaning of the task, e.g. rote learning times tables or using jingles as an aide memoire. Very often the jingle is remembered long after the learning. One early years maths intervention programme (2000) asks children to memorise numbers up to 100 in a rhythmical, jingle kind of way. Certainly the children are enthusiastic and appear pleased by their success. The instigators of this approach claim that the 'understanding' of what the numbers mean will come later and more easily if sequences of numbers can be readily recalled. The scheme is in its infancy. It will be interesting to see if promoting technical mastery then understanding, rather than the two together, works.

Strategies to help

The ability to memorise appears to develop as children mature. Researchers who set out to understand how young children memorise, showed them a number of objects, covered them, then asked the children to remember as many as they could. The children made a random and very short list. The researchers then showed the children how grouping the objects into categories of, e.g. soft toys, pieces of fruit, could help them remember more things, and the children had several tries using this strategy. A little later however, these same children, despite having been more successful when they tried grouping, did not adopt this strategy again. The youngest children immediately started calling out objects they could recall with no thought as to any 'method'.

There was a developmental difference – the older children would recall the grouping strategy when reminded, but only after a time of guessing and being asked if they had not heard of a better way. Similarly with suggesting that memorising could be eased by rehearsal, i.e. repeating the names or numbers over and over as most adults do when trying to commit phone numbers or birthdays or shopping lists to memory! Even when the children found this successful on one occasion there was no guarantee that they would remember it or try it again. Perhaps this links to Trevarthen's theory of there being 'critical' times when children learn specific things more easily. Perhaps it reinforces the point that very young children need time to mature and develop learning competences. Certainly there can be moments when suddenly and unexpectedly, the children grasp what was incomprehensible just a moment before.

Another 'special skill' is building a range of problem-solving strategies so that when a problem is encountered, children can select the most appropriate and effective way of solving it. Flavell (1985) called this process of making children aware of the different strategies possible, metacognition, or in other words, making them aware of how they were learning. This sounds very helpful – if children are made aware of what they do and what they could do, surely they will use the more successful way? The snag is that alerting children to a successful problem-solving strategy is a far cry from getting them to select it when a similar problem arises. This is why transfer of learning from one situation to another doesn't readily occur, even although it is difficult to understand why not. Perhaps if it did, then bad habits would not develop.

How often do we continue to do things despite knowing that there is a better way? My own 'blind spot' is to start playing the piano without checking the key signature. I know this is ridiculous but I do it again and again. Another is failing to take down exact details of references when quoting from other writings. Despite lots of tedious times hunting for sources which should have been noted at the time,

I can still let ideas take over and fail to record enough detail to complete bibliographies. This means another frustrating search! And so adults can be guilty of the same omissions as children. However, if teachers persevere and help children decide on the most useful problem-solving strategy for the problem at hand and make the links between different learning experiences explicit so that the children can identify the common features and understand how learning can be transferred from one task to the next, hopefully they will gradually come to be more thoughtful in their approach to the way they learn and thus do so more efficiently.

This kind of approach, i.e. looking at the abilities which underlie learning and helping their development, is one which concentrates on the process of learning. It depends on understanding children's development so that 'normal' progress, i.e. what children can be expected to be able to do at different stages, is understood, and on skilled and careful observation of the children's method of tackling an activity, so that the most helpful kind of intervention can be planned. Furthermore, parents and teachers can help by setting up the kind of learning activities which will take children's understandings forward. Activities which house potential problems need to be conceptualised so that ways of solving the problems can be discussed. In the early years, problem-solving experiences could be having the children set a table for four people from a cupboard of assorted dishes and cutlery, choosing musical instruments to produce a sound like rain to accompany a story or arranging groceries purchased at the 'shop' so that they would not be crushed on the way home. The term 'problem' need not mean something hugely complicated – just learning to cope with everyday occurrences can be the most useful problem-solving activity of all. More subtle learning is implicit in such activities, e.g. how do I know when it is my turn to go for snack and how do I remember the order of things I have to do first? This may seem a trivial issue but to children who have difficulty planning their day, and 8–10% of them do, then this is a major hurdle and requires as much careful help as any other difficulty.

If parents and teachers understand what is involved in learning and give lots of problem-solving opportunities, they can help their children to be more efficient and successful learners. Claxton (1990) again referring to his 'special skills' claims that, 'it is the development of these special skills rather than the level of some hypothetical ability which counts for much of the variance in school success.'

I hope that the following examples of play corners (Figures 1.2 to 1.9) will demonstrate how real learning is embedded in play. Once the learning potential is clear, it becomes easier to devise problem-solving opportunities and consider what kind of help would best suit individual children.

Understanding what is possible allows teachers to plan to allow it to happen. During the course of Wood and Bennett's research (1997), teachers changed 'choosing time' to 'planning time'. Although this could be viewed as semantics,

Social Development

- Working cooperatively – setting a table, preparing meals for others
- Talking on the telephone, turn taking, being pleasant and helpful
- Acting out roles, recognising lead roles, subservient roles
- Tidying, being responsible
- Coping with disagreements and reaching a compromise

Perceptual-motor Development

- Preparing meals – setting places at the table carefully
- Dressing the doll, fitting small garments, doing up buttons
- Tidying up, balancing dishes,
- Dialling the telephone
- Making a meal
- Dressing up

Home Corner

Emotional Development

- Acting out different roles – appreciating the nuances of each, e.g. caring for baby, learning to pretend
- Preparing a matching table – choice of dishes, tablecloth, colour, shape. Appreciation of presentation and 'looking good'
- Selecting suitable clothes for doll either in terms of weather or fashion
- Making a meal – appreciating what is needed for each meal

Intellectual Development

- Talking on the telephone, making suggestions, imagining responses
- 1 – 1 correspondence (is there a plate for every doll?)
- Planning and making a meal – choosing ingredients for healthy eating
- Language, e.g. responding to suggestions, giving alternative ideas, listening to others, making suggestions, learning new words
- Solving problems with a partner or in a small group

Figure 1.2 Learning in the home corner

Social Development

- Cooperating with each other to compose a tune

- Listening and waiting for turns

- Sharing instruments

- Talking with friends and adults about the music

Perceptual-motor Development

- Coordination – two hands working together to play instruments

- Rhythmical training, keeping the beat

- Controlling length of sound

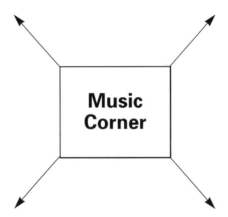

Emotional Development

- Investigating and appreciating different sounds

- Responding to sounds (movement, language)

- Understanding how sounds can represent ideas, e.g. fire crackling, rain pattering

- Selecting words to describe sounds

Intellectual Development

- Recognising sounds made by different instruments

- Counting the beat

- Learning the names of the instruments

- Learning words of songs

- Basic composition

- Planning what comes next

Figure 1.3 Learning in the music corner

Social Development

- Co-operating/discussing a patient's illness

- Development of altruism through caring for someone else

- Working together to discuss how to cope, what is to be done, how news is to go home

- Being responsible for someone else

Psychomotor Development

- Handling small equipment

- Rolling bandages

- Dialling the telephone

- Gently handling a sore arm/leg/head!

- Placing a stethoscope or hypodermic!

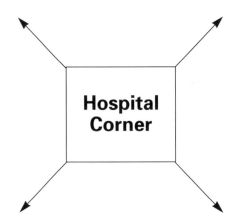

Hospital Corner

Emotional Development

- Role play – appreciation of different personnel

- Appreciating hospital procedures

- Respecting/understanding disability

- Confronting the idea of dying

Intellectual Development

- Learning about medicines

- Safety awareness

- S.O.S. awareness

- New 'hospital' vocabulary

Figure 1.4 Learning in the hospital corner

Social Development

- Taking turns

- Sharing puzzles

- Waiting

- Cooperating with a friend/in a small group

Perceptual-motor Development

- Fine motor skill development lifting and placing puzzle pieces with pincer grip

- Throwing dice – judging strength, timing of release

- Crossing the midline to place pieces

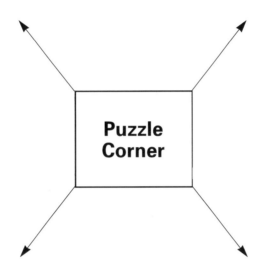

Puzzle Corner

Emotional Development

- Appreciation of shapes and colours to complete a pattern

- Satisfaction through completing a puzzle

- Matching colours and designs

Intellectual Development

- Matching shapes, finding strategies to complete puzzle

- Concentrating to complete puzzle

- Language development (e.g. describing shapes and pictures)

Figure 1.5 Learning in the puzzle corner

Social Development

- Discussing with adults and peers

- Cooperating/sharing ideas

- Sharing equipment

- Taking turns

Perceptualmotor Development

- Controlling – paintbrush, pencils, pens, sponges, glue spreader

- Hand – eye coordination

- Creating a pattern/design

- Placing textures (collage)

- Crossing the midline (to draw rainbow patterns)

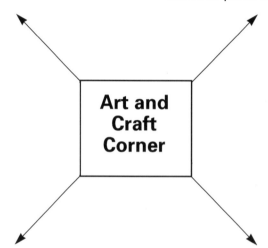

Art and Craft Corner

Emotional Development

- Making choices, e.g. which colour to use and why

- Appreciating the pattern

- Expressing ideas and thoughts onto paper

- Experiencing different textures (gluk, play doh, materials) on fingers

- Using symbols to express ideas

- Sense of achievement

Intellectual Development

- Learning colours and their names

- Mixing colours to make another one

- Language – children describing their pictures

- Sharing their ideas

Figure 1.6 Learning in the art and craft corner

Social Development

- Talking with adults and peers

- Sharing tools and toys

- Acting out roles with small world toys, diggers, etc.

- Waiting for turns

Psychomotor Development

- Using spade to fill bucket, dig holes and pat sand

- Use bucket to make sand castles

- Finger strengthening – making 'roads'/patterns in wet sand

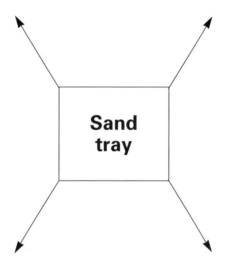

Sand tray

Emotional Development

- Appreciation of feel and texture of sand

- Using suitable tool for jobs

- Satisfaction from cooperation, e.g. making a fort and moat together

Intellectual Development

- Measuring, counting spadefuls

- Weighing language, e.g. empty, full, heavy, light

- Wet/dry sand properties of e.g. dry, runny sand to pour; wet, sticky sand to build

- More than, less than – conceptual development

Figure 1.7 Learning in the sand tray

Social Development

- Conveying ideas to one another
- Cooperating to carry out plan
- Being prepared to take role, e.g. bus driver or passenger

Perceptual-motor Development

- Handling chosen materials
- Gluing/painting
- Supporting boxes to make fantasy items

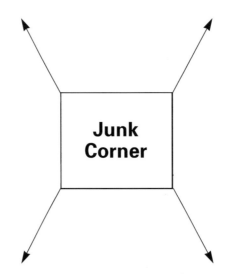

Junk Corner

Emotional Development

- Appreciating the possible outcome
- Weighing up different possibilities and choosing
- Pretending e.g. that the spaceship has taken off

Intellectual Development

- Conceptualising ideas
- Making decisions
- Planning the stages of putting the object together

Figure 1.8 Learning in the junk corner

Social Development

- Waiting, taking turns

- Cooperating (e.g. on see-saw)

- Working with/avoiding others

Perceptual-motor Development

- Running, climbing, balancing – all gross motor skills

- Throwing and catching, kicking – all ball skills

- Crawling up and down, on and off

Outdoor Play on Large Apparatus

Emotional Development

- Contributing to self-esteem

- Confidence in meeting new challenges

- Release of stress, e.g. in running freely

Intellectual Development

- Learning to balance

- Judging how much strength/speed/momentum is needed

- Planning the sequence of movement

Figure 1.9 Learning to move on large apparatus

there was a significant shift in their attitude towards free play. They anticipated what could happen, i.e. to a greater extent than before, and this allowed them to plan interventions. Planning like this also allows opportunities to fulfil the requirements of curriculum guidelines, e.g. to build in opportunities for children to gain 'knowledge and understanding of the world' by substituting wider topics in the corners, e.g. mini beasts cooking for snacks using the food different groups of children have and enjoy.

In each of these corners (Figures 2–9) potential learning scenarios have been described. Each corner holds many competences and children won't achieve them in the order they are written. However they can form the basis of assessment sheets. Those observing need to concentrate on particular aspects which are relevant to the children being assessed, either informally for practice for the observer, or more formally so that the observations contribute to a record of the child's progress, or indeed the child's individual needs. Such profiles can be shared with parents, with the class teacher who will have the child at the next stage or, with the parents' permission, they could be used as evidence to prove to the authorities that a child needs an assessment for physiotherapy or any other special kind of help.

Finally, providing the resources and stimulating ideas doesn't always mean that children will participate in the way that was intended. Wood and Bennett's (1997) research found that:

> children ignored the role-play context and developed their own themes which were repeated daily – 'babies and dogs' in one class where the area was resourced for a birthday party and in the shop 'guard dogs and burglars' was the preferred theme.

The teachers were in a dilemma. If they intervened they could spoil the children's own ideas and satisfaction in generating ideas and plans, but if they stood back, what was to become of all their planning for thematic or cross-curricular activities? Perhaps they had to judge the quality of what the children were doing in terms of commitment and inclusion and analyse the learning to find exactly what was being achieved. If this was pleasing, then the answer was to be flexible and leave their own planned outcome for another day. If the children's play was on the point of breaking down or just one or two players were dominating, with others disenchanted, then planning interventions which would swing the learning back to the original plan might be the best solution all round.

Intervention

When to intrude and when to let be, is a very difficult decision. We need to know when it is beneficial, even when it is likely to be accepted. Perhaps some questions and answers will help.

Why intervene?	To help the children who are having difficulty in playing well, i.e. happily and beneficially. To extend the children's learning.
When is the best time?	When the children themselves indicate that there is a need.
How should it be done?	Gently and sensitively when you have had time to realise the kind of intervention that is best.
Are there any special times?	When children are aggressive to other children or their games. When safety rules need to be reestablished. When children are distressed.

Figure 1.10 Times to intervene

You may be surprised that most of the answers in Figure 1.10 signal 'Unless you are sure you can help, and implicitly that you are needed, keep out!' Unfortunately, many adults can't resist butting in – they are sure to feel guilty if they don't because they are wiser, and they have information to pass on, don't they? or maybe they are being paid and they feel obliged to do something? or maybe it's too difficult to believe that children can do better on their own. It can be very hard for adults to relinquish the 'power' of being in charge, to stay back and give the children time to think out ways of playing for themselves – to trust the children not to waste time. A perplexed four-year-old once asked me, 'What is valuable time?' Obviously he had been found guilty of wasting it!

It's a good question, come to think of it. 'What is valuable time?': Time that could be better spent doing something else? But why should children change to do something else if they are interested in what they are doing? They are playing, after all! And what if they are, in the adults' eyes, wasting time? Why should they not? There's plenty left! And maybe children and adults need a change from busyness and bossiness. Maybe to enjoy being content and at peace is the most 'valuable' thing they will ever learn to do.

However, children differ in the support they need to take their understanding forward, and teachers who have analysed play to identify the many opportunities for learning are anxious that children benefit from them all. Thus they acknowledge that, 'if play provides valuable contexts for learning, it must also provide valuable opportunities for teaching.' (Wood and Bennett 1997) and they plan teaching interventions based on contextual knowledge, i.e. what the children are playing at, and how the content matches their potential for new learning. There are subtle nuances which have to be observed before intervening in play episodes. Observers may see what the children are doing, but not realise that they are involved in pretence. Intervening without this understanding can bring the play from pretence to reality, and the play is spoiled.

Also necessary is timing knowledge, i.e. recognising when the children's ideas are beginning to flag or when an opportunity to take the children forward appears. Then the intervention can be relevant and meaningful without overruling what the children are doing. It could be a very simple non-verbal intervention, e.g. placing another size of scoop in the sand (to aid measuring and weighing); it could be much more extensive, perhaps selecting a story which links to the game the children have made and during the reading asking them for ideas about how the characters would act or how the storyline could continue. The size and the scale of any intervention would depend on how engrossed the children were in what they were doing and how much new understanding could be interjected at one time.

CHAPTER 2

Studying play from a developmental perspective

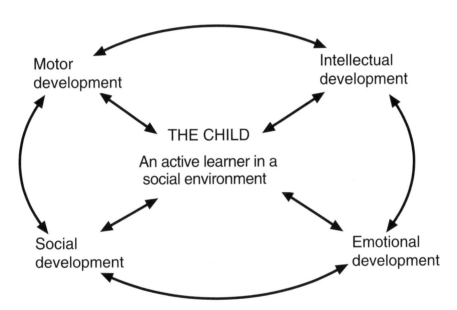

Figure 2.1 Aspects of development

The study of play and that of child development naturally complement each other. Those who seek to understand early child development can find many examples of each aspect of development in play, for 'as in the focus of a magnifying glass, play contains all the developmental tendencies in a condensed form' (Vygotsky 1978), and because it does, it is helpful to have a structure which can make this complex study more manageable. The one suggested here is to subdivide the study of development into four aspects, namely:

1. Social development, or the study of how children build relationships and learn to interact in groups,
2. Perceptual-motor development, or the study of how children learn to move efficiently and effectively in different environments,
3. Intellectual or cognitive development, or the study of how children learn to be logical and rational thinkers, and lastly,
4. Emotional or affective development, or the study of how children's feelings and perceptions affect their behaviour and learning.

Of course the four aspects interact and so progression or indeed regression in one aspect impinges on all of the others.

For example, a boy just able to swim will have taken a huge stride forward in the perceptual-motor domain, but progress also spills over into the others. Now that he is able to swim, he can interact with friends, a social gain; he has learned the names of different strokes and when they are best used, i.e. an intellectual gain; and possibly best of all, he has become more confident in his own ability to learn a new skill and this is an emotional gain.

The arrows in Figure 2.1 linking the different subdivisions of development are there to remind those who observe children, assess their progress and plan learning activities on that basis, that progress in one area is likely to benefit other areas as well. In a similar vein, new or unhappy experiences can cause children to regress to an earlier developmental stage. Then they will appear unable to do something which they had mastered before. This explains why parents can be flummoxed to find that their toilet-trained youngster has been having accidents in his new school! This may be a more common occurrence as more three-year-olds come into nursery, especially as being toilet trained is no longer one of the criteria for entry!

It can be difficult at times to know where to place different assessments. If a child is able to get dressed after P.E. in an acceptable amount of time where previously that was really difficult, what kind of progress is that? Is it intellectual? (the child can now understand the order of putting clothes on and gauge the time to be spent on each action), is it perceptual-motor? (the child has now developed the coordination to be able to do up buttons and tie laces), is it emotional? (the child has gained confidence from not being last). In my view, considering progress across the spectrum and weighing up all the advantages is more important than recording observations in the 'correct' place. In fact, different viewpoints can form the basis of rich discussions about children's progress.

And sometimes, just as different people have different reasons for doing things, so children can put greatest value on the less obvious benefits, e.g. 'When I can swim I'll be allowed to go to the pool without Mum!' This child is eager to be free!

A more detailed look at the rationale for choosing these aspects of development as key contributors to learning follows.

Social development

Many parents and teachers would say that the social dimension of learning is the most important one because if children are happy in school they are likely to be more receptive and confident and therefore able to take new learning on board, or at least they will not be afraid to ask for help. Moreover, sociable children are able to interact and learn from their peer group as well as from their parents and teachers. Many important researchers (e.g. Wells, Wood) emphasise the importance of active children learning in a social setting. Vygotsky's (1978) concept of 'the zone of proximal development' and Bruner's (1966) idea of 'scaffolding' both claim that if children are supported by more knowledgeable others as they learn – and these need only be one step ahead – they will be able to move forward more quickly than if they tried to learn alone.

Social development is therefore vitally important as it enables children to:

- learn from others,
- interact appropriately with adults and children,
- cooperate in group situations,
- take the lead role in decision making,

- at times take the subsidiary role,
- become aware that others also have needs,
- learn to empathise, i.e. understand different perspectives,
- understand how events affect others,
- develop socially acceptable behaviour in different circumstances,
- make decisions (social and/or moral) and stay with them,
- appreciate the value of friendship,
- develop altruism, i.e. caring for others at some cost to oneself.

Perceptual-motor development

The perceptual-motor aspects of development concern the acquisition of practical skills through developing abilities such as coordination, balance, strength and speed of movement. The underlying skills of planning movements so that they are efficient and effective, involve much perceptual learning based on making spatial and kinesthetic decisions. These depend on the other senses (i.e. visual, auditory and tactile), interpreting environmental cues accurately, so that feedback into the sensory system guides decisions about when to move, what to move and where to go!

Planning movement, that 'knowing what to do when', is also known as ideation. Large movements involving the large muscle groups are known as gross motor skills while the smaller muscle groups contribute to fine motor control.

N.B. If children have a learning difficulty, it can often be spotted first in poor movement coordination.

Example
Children who don't crawl very often can't crawl. As a result they lack early sequencing and coordination practice, and experience in stretching forward and making spatial decisions while in a secure position. Picture a child in a prone kneeling position, i.e. ready to crawl. Imagine one hand stretching forward to go into the movement. As this happens the body weight must shift to be completely supported by the other three points. This is good practice for learning to balance. If children don't experience this, and parents not understanding may be pleased that their children have 'jumped a stage', they are missing out a fundamental stage in learning to move effectively in different environments, for balance is essential to stability in both stillness and movement.

Often children who haven't crawled have reading difficulties, sometimes dyslexia. This is because they have missed out on sequencing practice, i.e. moving their limbs in the correct order imprinting a pattern of sequential movement into their brain. These omissions are also regularly found in children with dyspraxia (Macintyre 2000).

It is important that due attention is given to perceptual-motor development, because this enables children to:

- control their movements with increasing dexterity,
- move effectively and safely in different environments,
- develop spatial and kinesthetic awareness,
- develop the abilities that underlie skilled performance,
- know how to organise sequences of movement,
- become involved in health giving activities,
- enjoy participating in sports, gymnastics and dance,
- be confident in tackling new movement challenges.

Intellectual development

The intellectual, or cognitive aspects, of development concern the acquisition of knowledge and understanding about all aspects of everyday life and in all areas of the curriculum. Children need to develop this so that they can learn:

- to develop knowledge and understanding of the world,
- to develop language and communication skills,
- to develop the capacity to think logically and rationally,
- to make informed decisions,
- to develop mathematical and scientific concepts,
- to solve problems,
- to think creatively about new ways of doing things,
- to concentrate on the task at hand,
- to cope with specialised learning in the classroom and at home.

Emotional development

This is perhaps the most difficult area to understand, possibly because the development of confidence as one example, is only apparent in carrying out another task or perhaps in changed non-verbal behaviour which is always difficult to assess. Other things like appreciation or imagination are less tangible than, e.g. getting a sum right and making progress in mathematics, but this is a hugely important aspect of development for it allows children to:

- pretend to be someone else,
- approach new situations with confidence,

- express feelings and emotions,
- cope with anxieties and be more resilient,
- enjoy open-ended problems,
- appreciate works of art/music/dance,
- cry if they want to,
- understand the perception of other people,
- develop altruism,
- appreciate the atmosphere e.g. in a church,
- be innovative and imaginative.

As all of this terminology becomes clear, there are two other very important factors to remember. First, one aspect of change may be dominant at one time and affect the others. Think of sudden growth spurts. At these times children who have grown have to make physical and emotional adjustments especially if they are 'the first' in their peer group. The children who are waiting to grow have similar hurdles and the emotional upheaval can act negatively on other aspects of learning. Growing children all pass through the same stages but the pace of so doing is different and this can cause anguish and uncertainty. Perhaps this is particularly true in the early years when parents are apt to make comments, such as 'He's very shy,' or comparisons which the listening child interprets as criticisim e.g. 'Goodness, isn't he big, much bigger than my boy.' It is not hard to imagine the impact on the child's self-esteem!

Second, the children at the centre of all of this are not passive recipients, but people who make decisions and react to teaching in their own way. Children always surprise by how much they can learn but they will bring their own experiences and be influenced by their genetic endowment and their context – their previous learning, their environment and the quality and quantity of the opportunities they have had. Perhaps they will learn best if their own ways are recognised and respected.

> Each child is an unique individual. Each brings a different life story to the early years setting. Growing up as a member of a family and community with unique ways of understanding the world creates an individual pattern and pace of development.   (Scottish Consultative Council on the Curriculum 1998)

This being so, parents, teachers and nursery nurses must understand that there are key factors interacting to influence development and how children learn. They are heredity, growth, maturation and environment (Figure 2.2) and will be considered in turn.

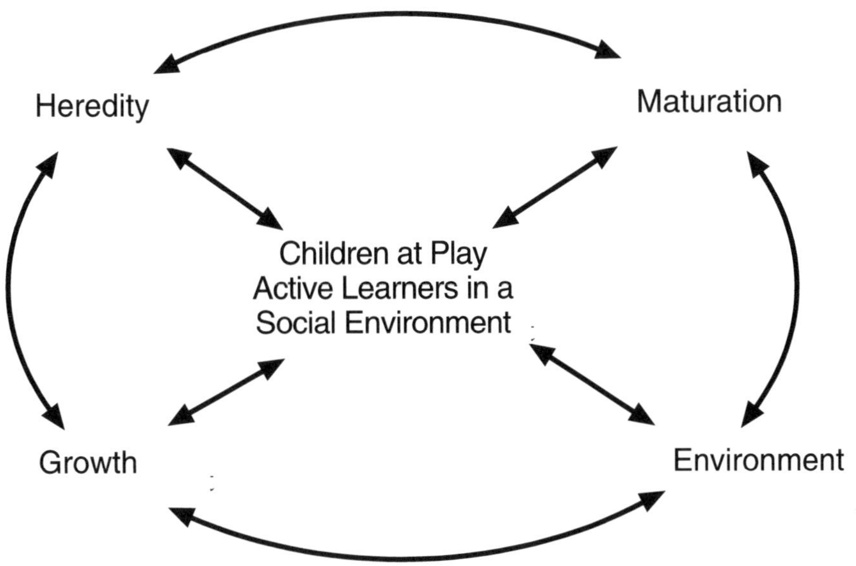

Figure 2.2 Influences on development

Heredity

Bee (1999) describes heredity as 'a genetic blueprint which influences what we can do.' The influence of the nature (inherited/genetic) component of development against that of the nurture (environmental) one has been hotly debated for many years. The conclusion has always been that a constant and complex interplay of both factors determines the child's behaviour. Nonetheless, trying to understand the starting-off position, i.e. what the child has inherited, and how home and preschool, i.e. environmental influences, have shaped a child's attitude towards play and learning, is a fascinating study. And of course it is essential if we are to understand if and how we can help children build on the favourable aspects of both.

Where does it all begin?

Unless there is some genetic abnormality, e.g. in Down's Syndrome, the nucleus of each cell in the body has 46 chromosomes arranged as 23 pairs. These hold all the genetic pointers for each individual and determine the factors shown in the following list:

- height,
- aspects of personality, e.g. temperament,

- body build,
- patterns of physical development,
- vulnerablity to allergies,

- aspects of intelligence, e.g. the ability to empathise with other people's feelings,

- possibly dyslexia and/or dyspraxia.

The only cells which do not contain 46 chromosomes are the sperm and ovum. They are known as gametes. Each has 23 chromosomes, not 23 pairs. Each chromosome is composed of a chain of molecules of a chemical (DNA) which can be subdivided into genes and each gene is responsible for an aspect of development, e.g. which blood group, what hair colour or even what diseases the child inherits. At conception the 23 chromosomes from the father and 23 from the mother come together. They can hold similar 'instructions' or very different ones. Researchers are still trying to explain the part each plays when different instructions come together. If, for example, a child inherits one which signals 'shyness' (a temperamental trait) from one parent and 'outgoingness' from the other, what then? Bee (1999) explains that typically, one gene will be dominant and this will influence the child's behaviour while the other, the recessive gene is dormant and has no visible effect. However, this dormant gene can still be passed on to the next generation.

These are 'either/or' characteristics, there is no blend. This explains why children in the same family, brought up in the same environment can be 'chalk and cheese' with parents amazed at the very different characteristics the children display. Even when two siblings look alike, they can still have very different temperaments – one may be happy-go-lucky and resilient and appear to weather storms unscathed, while the other is sensitive and vulnerable and has a harder time coping in what, to the outsider, would be seen was the same set of circumstances. Of course the siblings may learn from one another and behaviours can be altered by copying or modelling, but fundamentally the temperaments stay different because they depend on inherited genetic material. At the same time the inherited genes do not absolutely determine the pattern of any child's development. In Bee's (1999) words 'they influence what can be done.' The specific set of instructions contained in the genes is known as the genotype whereas the phenotype is the name given to the child's observed characteristics. Figure 2.3 shows that both the genotype and the environment influence the phenotype. Additionally they also work together to further influence the phenotype.

Example

A mum-to-be may conceive a child with genotype 'high IQ', however unwise use of drugs or alcohol during pregnancy may damage the child's nervous system so that the initial potential cannot be realised. These damaging environmental effects are called teratogens. Others are rubella in early pregnancy which may result in sight, hearing

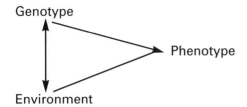

Figure 2.3 Influences on the phenotype

or heart problems, or AIDS (although only 25% of babies born to mothers with full blown AIDS, as opposed to HIV will develop the disease). Viruses can also attack the placenta reducing the nutrients which sustain the embryo.

Distinct from teratogens are genetic errors. One example is the chromosome abnormality which results in Down's Syndrome which holds a degree of intellectual retardation as well as particular physical characteristics. Another is phenylketonuria, a metabolic disorder which cannot be detected prenatally and which prevents the metabolism of a common amino acid. Treatment is a rigid diet, essential to prevent the onset of mental retardation. These errors occur at the moment of conception and are permanent although new technology may be able to change this. Most people will regard this as a most welcome intervention.

Personality factors or temperamental traits are other inherited factors, but they may be more amenable to environmental influence.

Example

If a child inherits the temperamental trait 'impulsiveness' and so tends to act without considering the consequences, then a home and school setting which models 'slowing down' and thinking through the outcomes of actions could be very beneficial. If, for example, adults help the child practise 'crossing the road drill', calmly pointing out the dangers, then later the child may be less likely to dive into the road. Of course one example won't do much to change usual ways of behaving. Constant and consistent examples are needed to influence temperamental traits which house relatively enduring characteristics. Although children may well learn to slow down in familiar situations, when new ones arise, they tend to instinctively respond in their own temperamental way. Impulsivity does tend to diminish as children mature, and this together with the learning which comes from daily experiences means that they can be 'trusted to be safe' and need less supervision as they play.

An impulsive child in a household of impetuous adults however, has no different role model and will have a harder time becoming reflective and cautious.

At the other end of the impulsive continuum is 'reflectiveness' and generally this is seen as a welcome trait. People who are reflective take time to consider options and therefore often choose the best one. Taken to the extreme of course, these individuals can be confused by visualising too many alternative ways and never get anything done! There are times when snap decisions need to be made and other times when there is time to make an informed choice. Maybe the skill comes in recognising which is which.

Understanding development in this way is important, for theoretical knowledge houses practical implications. Realising, for example, that parents with higher IQs are likely to pass on the wherewithal to do well in school *and* provide a stimulating learning environment, means that less-favoured children are doubly disadvantaged. This knowledge can justify early intervention programmes specifically designed to overcome the double deficit (both genetic and environmental) which less fortunate children face. If this happens early, children can begin primary school on a more level playing field. Without this understanding, teachers could expect children with very different backgrounds and experiences to learn the same things together and this could further compound the inequalities.

While growth and maturation are sometimes used as synonyms they are subtly different.

Growth

Growth is a change in quantity, for example, the increased size of the body with age or the number of words in a child's vocabulary or the range of skills a child has. In other words growth denotes change in a quantitive, descriptive way. It says 'this is what occurred', but provides no description of why.

Of course, these growth changes have associated psychological changes. Young children usually want to be big because they associate this with being clever or independent or grown up. Moreover, researchers in schools have found that teachers give more responsibility and independence to children who are big for their age. They appear to consider size as an indicator of competence rather than chronological age, even over ability. Or perhaps they consider that they need to protect the wee ones more. Bee (1999) certainly claims that 'large and robust children elicit different kinds of care giving than fragile ones.' For whatever reason 'big' children appear to be seen as being 'ready' or more reliable earlier and they are given more complex tasks. Usually they respond well and the parents' and teachers' expectations are met.

Large children are also more likely to be chosen as leaders by their peer group (Lerner 1985). This is important even in the earliest years, for the tallest boys and girls can be six inches taller than the smallest ones. Perhaps realising this, i.e. the tendency to favour one group, parents, teachers and nursery nurses can help the smaller children by remembering that size does not always equal competence and ensure that responsibilities are more equally given out.

Heredity has a very strong influence on growth. When healthy children have supportive environments, their genetic influence explains their height. Tall parents usually have tall children, while short parents have shorter ones, although there is some regression to the mean. Furthermore, children can't eat to be tall or starve to be short as many an aspiring jockey or ballerina has discovered. However, growth rate can be affected if the environment is really poor because malnutrition or abuse does cause the growth rate to drop. Some recurring illnesses such as asthma can also affect growth. The effects of regular medication on growth are being investigated at this time.

Estimating final height

The final height of children can be predicted with some accuracy. The correlation between height at age two and final height is .78 (Tanner 1990). However, this works best for children of parents of average height. The calculation will need amending with two tall parents or two small ones. Length at birth has a much lower correlation, only .3 because conditions in the womb, i.e. environmental influences, have a strong effect. The timing of puberty also affects final height. Those who go through it early tend to be shorter. And so although the genetic influence in growth patterning is strong, there are other factors which need to be considered (Table 2.1).

Table 2.1

Children who reach their height potential, tend:	Children who do not reach their height potential, tend:
to come from an 'advanced' background to have consistent security and support to have escaped illnesses such as asthma necessitating drug therapy	to come from a disadvantaged background to have erratic support to have been laid low by illnesses to be from larger families

A combination of factors – genetic/environmental and personal work together to influence height.

Maturation

The term maturation means 'genetically programmed patterns of change' (Gesell 1925). These include changes in body size and shape, muscle control and hormonal changes at puberty. These patterns are genetically programmed, they are inbuilt. They begin at the moment of conception and continue until death. Understanding these changes is important because they explain development rather than describe it.

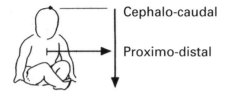

Figure 2.4 Early physical developmental

All children in all cultures pass through the same patterns of change. Physical development is cephalo-caudal (i.e. progressing from head to toe), and proximodistal (i.e. progressing from the centre to the periphery). This is why babies can hold their heads up before their back muscles are strong enough to let them sit, and why they can sit before they are able to pull up to stand. Most children crawl, even up stairs before they walk, for this is the same action. The instructions for these sequences are built in at the moment of conception, they are not taught. Even anxious parents can't teach their children to walk. They won't walk till they are 'ready', i.e. till they have the strength and balance and coordination, and the maturity to allow them to try. The fact that most children walk between 11 and 18 months establishes one detail in a timetable of age-norms and this is often used as an assessment device to measure progress. For example see Table 2.2. It must be remembered however that the span of 'normal' development is wide.

Maturation and perceptual development

For many years it was thought that genetically determined development was preset regardless of the environment. One interesting phenomenon which appeared to support this was the child's developing language. Many develop strange past tense word forms, e.g. 'I goed to bed', despite never having heard such usage. However it is now accepted that maturation is enhanced by a stimulating environment. Sadly, children from severely impoverished environments do not develop the same density of neural connections in the brain as those who have rich experiences, such as interacting with people who are interested in children and who encourage them to learn. Trevarthen (1993) claimed that these must happen at the right times 'when the brain is thirsting for new experiences', if they are to be readily assimilated.

There are also social and cultural differences which impact on maturation. Being allowed, or being constrained, to do certain things at certain times, e.g. getting out to play unsupervised, going to nursery at age three, 'big' school at age five in Britain, and not until seven in Germany, i.e. at an age when the authorities decide it is the best time to begin formal education. These socialising events accompany the biological/maturational changes which occur. Again, the effects of heredity and environment work together to influence the individual development of children.

Table 2.2 Developmental Norms

Age 6–8 months	– should be able to reach and grasp, but still will have difficulty 'letting go' – should be 'nearly sitting' unsupported for a short time – may be rolling over sideways
Age 9–12 months	– pulling up on furniture, attempting to stand with support – will be moving around – hopefully crawling
Age 1 year – 18 months	– walking and crawling intermittently – lots of bumping down Some will scribble using a finger thumb pencil grip but often a clutched grip is used. No hand dominance at this stage.
Age 2 years	– immature running pattern evident now – may be little control in stopping Climbs stairs in a step feet together pattern. Can unscrew lids, thread beads and chat in longer phrases. Understands what is being said. Will rebel if displeased! Shows clear hand preference although some jobs can still be done with either hand.
Age 3 years	– confident running now. Jumping to have 2 feet off the ground still difficult. Combines movements e.g. running to kick a ball – not always successfully. Attempts stairs with the mature fluent pattern. Catches a large soft ball.
Age 4 years	– pedals a trike now. Can run and jump to land on two feet. Can pour juice from a jug and wipe dishes. Can hammer nails and do jig-saws. Has a large vocabulary. Still concerned with 'own' events rather than appreciating other people's but developing altruism and empathy especially if role models are at hand.
Age 5 years	– can skip and follow a clapping rhythm now. Enjoys stories and rhymes. Likes to look after others and take responsibility. Likes to help organise and can tidy up. All the basic motor patterns should be achieved now.

N.B.   the 'normal' age span for the development of the basic movement patterns is wide, but children markedly different from their peers should be checked out to see if extra help is required.

Children who don't crawl may not have the sequencing and coordinator to allow them to do so. Instead of allowing them to miss this stage, crawling games and analysing the crawl pattern for the children can be helpful in giving the kind of balancing and reaching experience which they otherwise would have missed.

In comparison to the limited motor development which prevents very young babies from carrying out more than seemingly random, or uncoordinated movements, their perceptual development is quite advanced at birth. They can see, and are especially well-focused at about eight inches, which is nursing distance;

they can hear and recognise family sounds and can respond to these to ensure that their caretaking needs are met; they know their mother or their caretaker's smell, and can recognise this source of security; they can readily discriminate between the four basic tastes of sweet, sour, bitter and salty, and by making their preferences felt, they can ensure that they are given the correct kinds of food. With these capabilities in place they are all set for learning.

Observation of newborns allows researchers to claim that not only do they have these capacities, but they are able to make associations between them. Babies, hearing their mother's footsteps, for example, will begin the searching and sucking actions which precedes feeding. Likewise, if someone who usually plays with them approaches, they will open their eyes wide and by increasing the activity of their arms and legs, indicate that they too are ready to play. This is called schematic learning. The babies are building a repertoire of patterns or schemas from their experiences and using them to make judgements about their future behaviours. Rovee-Collier (1986) suggested that these kinds of linkages are in fact the development of expectancies in children, i.e. the beginnings of the process of intellectual development. Bandura (1992) also shows that, 'The development of memory skills helps children to remember what actions in what situations produced what outcomes.'

In this way children build a bank of information so that when they meet a new situation they can make judgements about the most appropriate response. Others may help the children in this decision-making process by providing reinforcements: smiling, nodding or other rewards which indicate that the demonstrated behaviour is approved.

Beyond the baby stage, the development of the different modes of perception has a marked influence on how children *can* learn, and this of course influences the best ways for them to be taught:

- Visual
- Auditory
- Tactile
- Kinesthetic
- Proprioceptive
- Vestibular

Visual

The most obvious benefit of vision is to be able to see clearly and recognise people and objects and the distances between them. To do this the eyes must work together with no condition, e.g. astigmatism or cataract, which could take objects out of focus and make any sort of spatial judgement difficult. If children have visual difficulties, they can be seen peering closely at their book, screwing up one eye to cut out distractors, even shaking their heads as if to clear away a foggy image. Sometimes opiticians may give children the 'all clear' because they can see ahead quite clearly and recognise letters instantly, however their functional vision can still be impaired. If it is, the letters on a page may wobble or run together, even jump out of sequence, making identification and reading difficult. These children are also likely to have difficulty in tracking objects, e.g. the path of an approaching ball. If they lose the flight path, then their fingers don't have time to make the necessary spatial adjustments to let them catch and the ball drops at their feet.

If the eyes don't follow the letters smoothly in the correct sequence, learning to read is bound to be problematic. Tracking difficulties may make it very difficult for children to identify 'which line' and 'where on the page' they should begin. In maths too, faulty tracking can cause figures to jump out of line, meaning that while the children understand what it is they have to do and can do it orally, getting the right answer on paper is a different story. When copying from the board is necessary, these children have real difficulties. Then, they have to find the correct place on the board, leave that, and then find the right place on their page, and perhaps do this several times in each lesson. Giving the children an inclined board can make a huge difference, because one of the adjustments, i.e. transcribing from the vertical to the horizontal and back, has been eased.

Another difficulty arises if the children have poor three dimensional vision. This means that they see objects flat against their background rather than protruding from it. As a result, the children's spatial judgements are impaired. They walk into things, get bumped and bruised and possibly even scolded at the same time. Very young children may not be able to see their shoes on a patterned carpet because they don't stand out. Any complex design is confusing. Tables at school need to be covered with plain cloth to ease identifying and sorting objects, e.g. jigsaws or matching shape puzzles. Finding hidden pictures in a background of other lines is impossible. It is not difficult to see why children who bump into things and feel clumsy and uncoordianted have associated confidence difficulties and feel misunderstood and sad.

Sometimes children with visual perception problems cannot bear their personal space to be invaded. They are extremely protective and become very upset if others come in too close. As they also misjudge distances, they can be upset by children who come too near and upset them, even when these others had no such intention.

A last word on visual perception concerns children whose vision does not cut out distractors. Their attention is constantly interrupted by movements in the environment, e.g. fluttering leaves, which others manage to ignore. They are often scolded for not paying attention when visual distractibility is the cause. Self-esteem is hit again!

Auditory

Hearing clearly allows children to be alert to everything that goes on in their environment. It is also the most important requisite for listening, and children who listen well have a good chance of learning well. Children who don't listen well give a late response to instructions and this can cause problems from the moment they rise till bedtime. The problem often is that these children can't cut out background noises. Most children do this filtering out automatically, and this lets them concentrate on the most important things being said. But those with auditory difficulties strain to hear through the rustle or the buzz that is going on around them and can become understandably tired and irritable as they do. Relief comes from switching off all noises, and when teachers say 'He is in a world of his own', maybe this is why. The other world is too frantically busy. And so these children miss the teacher's instructions and often have to follow a neighbour to catch up. Their responses are delayed and if the neighbour's actions are faulty, theirs are too.

Finding a quiet spot for them is not easy in a busy classroom and writing simple instructions rather than calling them out takes time. Establishing quite a rigid routine so that the children know what comes next is a great help. These quite simple moves to assist the children can be very productive in the improved quality of the response that is received. They also stop the frustration of having to repeat instructions over and over again.

Tactile

This is a less obvious source of trouble for some children. There are really three aspects to consider. The first is to understand that some children can't bear to be touched. Even inadvertently brushing against them can cause them to overreact, possibly hitting out. The second is that touch may cause children to jerk as in a reflex action. The children may be sitting quietly listening to a story when one with this sensitivity jerks and disrupts the quiet mood. The child can be just as surprised as you for what has happened is that a T-shirt has rubbed his back and caused a reflex, just like the knee jerk. This is beyond the child's control but he gets the blame! The third is that some children require what is called hard feedback from the environment. These children crash around. They don't know their own strength, and put far too much of it into every action. When they run they go too fast and can't stop unless they crash into a wall or anyone standing by; they press their pencil too hard and it breaks; things just come apart in their hands. They have difficulty in interpreting the feedback from the environment unless it is strong and to get this feedback they need to 'bang hard'.

Kinesthetic

Some children have little awareness of their bodies, i.e. kinesthetic awareness. They are not aware of the effect moving one body part has upon the others. They have difficulty moving just one part in isolation, with children under three especially tending to move the body as a whole instead of in separate parts. This is wasteful of energy and makes the movement appear clumsy and uncoordinated. They also tend not to be sure where they end and the outside world begins and this lack of a clear appreciation of body boundary makes fine movements, e.g. holding a pencil, difficult. Of course hands still tend to be chubby which can make refined actions problematic too. Gradually as the children mature the movements become more refined.

The kinesthetic sense can be subdivided into three parts:

1. Body awareness – Do I know where my feet are without looking? Can I feel how close my back is to the wall? Do I know how to push my hand through my sleeve?
2. Body boundary – Do I know where I end and the bat I have in my hand begins? Do I know how far I am from the edge of the pavement?
3. Spatial awareness – Can I judge how far the car is from the zebra crossing? Can I put the jug of juice on the table without knocking the edge and spilling the juice?

I hope these questions show how difficult the day is for children who have not a well developed sense of space and where they are in it. They get bumped and bruised and soon, because they have difficulty moving accurately and quickly, no one wants them to play.

Luckily young children love games which help develop body awareness, e.g. Simon says 'Put your hands on your heads', or use rhythmical phases, e.g. 'hands on heads, push them tall, hands on knees then curl up small'. These can gradually include elbows, knees and backs to enlarge the children's body awareness. This training all helps in activities like forward rolls, for how can children 'make a round back', if they can't feel where their back is? How can they be safe if they don't know how far they are from the wall?

Proprioceptive

The proprioceptor cells which are in the muscles and joints of the body work with the kinesthetic groups to tell where the body is in relation to outside objects. They help movement to be segmented and efficient. Children who have a sound proprioceptive sense can sit down without looking at their chair – they sense where it is, how high the seat is and so they can judge the amount of effort needed to sit down. They can do all their usual movement patterns without looking – fastening buttons, even tying laces can be done by feel alone. Those who can't must compensate by turning to see and/or bending to feel, i.e. movements which take time and need added coordination and concentration. Proprioceptors also help maintain balance and control, especially when different amounts of fluctuating strength are required, e.g. in bicycling over uneven grass instead of on a smooth pathway. Children with a poor proprioceptive sense are less skilled in these types of movements, and need to use their other senses, particularly visual, to compensate.

Vestibular

Vestibular receptors are situated in the inner ear and work to coordinate movements which require balance. This is why children with an ear infection sometimes find their sense of balance is affected. Some children just love to go on the waltzer at the fair; the whirling action temporarily confuses their proprioceptors and they feel giddy, almost out of control. They enjoy this sense of losing and regaining balance. Others find this kind of sensation unpleasant, to be avoided at all costs. But even those who seek this temporary sensation of vertigo would not wish to have it continuously, because then carrying out even everyday movements would be extremely stressful.

The vestibular sense responds to changes of position of the head, automatically coordinating the eyes and body. It also helps children recognise the midline of their bodies which is important in understanding directionality.

Environment

The child is born into a family system which may be nuclear, i.e. two parents and possibly brothers and sisters, or extended, i.e. including other relations like grandparents or longstaying friends, or transient, i.e. with different people arriving and departing at longer or shorter intervals. The child may be very important or not important at all to those who make up the group. The group itself may be stable, e.g. having the same sorts of values which stay the same over time so that the children gain a clear picture of what is 'right' and 'wrong' in that context, or the value systems may fluctuate like the people who come and go. The atmosphere in the group may be pleasant or filled with acrimony. And so you can understand how children come to school with very different expectations of security and awareness of the kind of behaviour which would be acceptable in a new setting.

The family in turn exists within a larger cultural system or community with different traditions, values and beliefs which may be more or less important to the smaller groups within it. Children absorbing the mores of their culture will expect staff to understand all the aspects of their different beliefs and value systems, e.g. to know and appreciate important festival days, or any food limitations or friendship patterns. Part of children's learning is to broaden their awareness of and come to respect different perspectives. They have a lot to learn.

Many complex questions about the effect of the quality and quantity of a child's environment are constantly being asked, e.g. to what extent does providing a rich stimulating environment in school compensate for deprivation at home and if it does, at what age does it need to be provided? Or, if this kind of environment is essential, how is it that so many highly successful people overcome severe disadvantages? Why is there the adage that a certain amount of disadvantage appears to spur some people to high levels of achievement? Does this depend on personality factors, e.g. grit and perseverance, or cultural factors, e.g. athletes being 'valued' and acting as role models for children who can practise without expensive equipment? Or have both positives to be in place if adversity is to be overcome? Is there a danger that children given everything on a plate as it were, will have nothing to work for? Or do humans always want something they do not have?

Those who provide education work hard to compensate for the disadvantages of both genetic and environmental deprivation that children encounter and no one would wish that any child was denied opportunities to flourish. The question of whether and to what extent a learning environment can compensate for a poor home environment is a difficult one to answer. Morally, children can't be denied access to a better learning environment for the sake of carrying out research to find out. Considering the level of disadvantage and the form it takes, the length and timing of any malnourishment or abuse adds to the complexity. Certainly the environmental factors are hugely complex just as the genetic ones are!

Moving now from more general considerations to more personal ones we find that the genetic factors which children inherit can, in turn, profoundly influence their environment. For instance children with sunny temperaments and smiling faces tend to receive more positive feedback than more sombre children. Children who spot any opportunities and go forward to take advantage of them tend to be favoured over those that are withdrawn and hold back. This shows how children themselves can positively or negatively affect their environment. Their own interactions, based on temperament as well as coping skills, significantly affect any outcome.

Long and Valiant (1984) studied 456 boys from inner-city schools and identified protective factors which appeared to overcome environmental disadvantages. They were:

- as preschoolers they had been affectionate, easy children
- they had a positive bond with at least one carer
- they had reasonable language and mathematical skills.

In other words they had some positives to begin with and these endured to help them.

A high-quality environment is a stable one where children have love and security and lots of appropriate stimulation. Given these circumstances, both resilient and vulnerable children are likely to do well. Resilient children can even do well in unfavourable circumstances. It is when vulnerable children have a poor environment that the outlook is bleak. The important issue is that neither a poor environment nor a vulnerable personality alone causes a poor outcome. The crippling factor is when the two negatives come together as a double blow.

It seems, however, that resilient children can do better than others in poor environments because they look forward rather than dwelling on things past. They recognise and seize opportunities. Perhaps knowing this, teachers and nursery nurses could help 'other' children by pointing out what possibilities there are. This links with helping the children plan rather than always concentrating on the thing that they are attempting to make.

What then are the implications within this nature/nurture debate? There is a lighter side and a darker side to this in my view. It is one thing for parents to note and enjoy mannerisms which they see passed on, or real or imagined potentials for achieving certain distinctions, provided they are realistic and do not stress the children or attempt to mould them into images of what their parents themselves would have liked to be. It is another if parents and teachers make poor prognoses about their children and justify their lack of input and encouragement on that basis. Time and time again children who are motivated surprise, sometimes amaze by their sustained commitment and their level of achievement, while others with seemingly greater gifts switch off and do not fulfil their potential at all. And so while the genetic endowment of individuals supplies a potential development, the fulfilment of this is facilitated by the kind of environment which provides stimulation and learning possibilities. Today, those who are concerned by the nature/nurture division usually say that it is most fruitfully seen as an interactive, interdependent process rather than a posing of opposites.

In the new century, one major intervention in the 'nature' field is genetic engineering, when the scientific modification of a baby's genetic code is possible. Identifying genetic disorders which cause severe illnesses or handicaps in the foetus leads to the complex questions which surround pre-natal intervention, even abortion. In a radio phone-in Mary Warnock, co-author of The Warnock Report (1978), pleaded that only parents of a child whose quality of life would be severely affected should be given the choice of having an abortion, while another mother of two healthy boys claimed that her desire for a girl was so strong that she would be prepared to abort a boy! When such possibilities exist, different people will obviously have very different views on the extent to which they should be able to determine the characteristics of their child, or indeed whether that child should be born at all.

As more and more children are spending time with childminders, at play groups and nurseries so the responsibility for much of the children's day is shifting. Children from very different environments are coming together earlier and for longer. Understanding how they develop and ensuring that learning opportunities 'match and extend' is therefore even more complex and more important than ever before.

CHAPTER 3

A closer look at social and emotional development

This chapter will examine the aspects of social and emotional development which are particularly relevant to young children at play. Under the social heading, the topics are the development of relationships with parents, interaction skills at home and school and the development of the gender concept. Under the emotional heading comes the interpretation of expressions, responding to expressions, developing empathy, and understanding pretence and fantasy.

The development of relationships

The earliest relationships are between babies and their parents. The term 'attachment' was conceptualised by Mary Ainsworth (1972), who identified and discussed the implications of the 'strong and long-lasting affectational tie formed between baby and parents.' Recognition of this bonding which occurred soon after birth (Klaus and Kennell 1976) prompted the change of practices which brought about-to-be-dads from the traditional pacing in the waiting room to the delivery room to share the birth process, and kept baby cots alongside the new-mums at all times instead of removing them to the nursery to give them time to sleep!

More recent research (Myers 1987) however, casts some doubt on the immediacy of this bonding which must comfort parents whose babies had to be in intensive care or for one reason or another were denied early cuddles. The strength of the bonding is now thought to depend more on the 'pattern of mutual interlocking attachment behaviours' (Bee 1995) which develops over the first weeks and months. As the parents and babies interpret each other's signals and respond to them, they each learn the kinds of behaviour which will please the other, e.g. holding eye contact, smiling, gurgling. As they do so, they build a repertoire of schemas, i.e. Piaget's patterns of behaviour (mental models) which form a baseline and facilitate decisions about future interactions. This communication, this mutuality, appears to underlie the security and satisfaction and pleasure with each other, which is bonding.

But does this always happen? Sometimes this bonding takes longer. Sometimes parents of very premature babies are afraid to become involved, fearing even greater distress should the baby die. The baby with feeding tubes and on a ventilator cannot be held and is unable to respond to the communications of the parents. When these babies do go home, the responsibility of nurturing such tiny infants can be overwhelming and tension can cause the wrong messages to be conveyed. Happily once these babies progress and catch up, the development of the attachment can catch up too. Blind babies are others who cannot participate in this mutuality . . . until the parents learn to read their different non-verbal cues and realise that compensatory behaviours, e.g. limb gestures, are communicating meaning in the same way as sighted infants signal with their eyes. Then the attachment is as strong as for any other child.

Some children just seem to be born with difficult temperaments. They show resistance to close contact, they have irregular sleeping and eating patterns, they cry a lot and they often refuse to be soothed. It is not difficult to imagine or remember the wear and tear on the parents and the effect on child–parent relationships. Some are able to persevere and all is well, but some feel a long-lasting resentment and the relationship never really gels. Parents with a difficult baby may feel they have failed to match society's image and their own expectations of what parenting is about; they feel guilty because they are not immediately flooded with parental love. Then low self-esteem is added to the stress, for the baby couldn't be to blame . . . or could it?

Some adults may find attachment behaviours very difficult, e.g. parents who are disappointed in their child, those who are poor and anticipate that another child will increase their difficulties, parents whose own relationships are foundering, parents who themselves did not benefit from a stable home and who may not have the experience or security to pass on to a child. One young mother who had abused her baby explained, 'I wanted someone to love me, but she didn't, she just cried, so I hit her.' No one would suggest that all abused parents in turn abuse their children, but if several disadvantages come together, e.g. inexperience, poverty, despair, with a crying baby, then it is more likely that children will be abused.

Happily, however, most children do build secure attachments with their parents and carers. This attachment can be intensely strong and can last throughout life providing mutual support for those involved. It can endure despite severe difficulties and even over long periods of separation.

Shaefer (1989) claims that the importance of this early social development cannot be over-stated for 'the establishment of the child's primary social relationships are generally considered to constitute the foundation on which all psychosocial behaviour is based.'

Certainly it has been found that securely attached youngsters persist longer at play activities. This may be because they are more content and confident in exploring their environment and this, in turn, stimulates intellectual development. Gradually, as they mature and meet different groups of people, children move from preferring solitary play to have the understanding which allows them to play with others, and 'by age three or four children prefer to play with others rather than alone' (Hartup 1992). This is not always an easy transition, in fact many early years' teachers would claim that much of their day is taken up with helping children to learn the social skills which make playing together possible. How do they do this? First they need to understand how prosocial behaviour develops so that they know what can reasonably be expected of children of different ages and from different backgrounds. They also need a repertoire of coping strategies and to understand the effect of their own modes of response.

Example

At nursery, Jake was a 'handful' – boisterous, loud, laughing but domineering, bossing the other children for most of the day. Although the teacher in charge urged the child to share toys and not to barge into the others, she did this tentatively and didn't follow her admonitions through . . . in fact her comments, e.g. 'You are a lively lad,' seemed to support the child and reinforce his behaviour. Moreover his uncontrolled behaviour was raising the tempo – other children were beginning to be 'lively' too! This inexperienced teacher didn't realise that being firm was different from being cruel and that she had to let the child know the difference between disliking him as a person and disliking his behaviour.

Pointing out how unacceptable behaviour affects other children is not always successful, especially if that level of empathy has not been developed, but the talking together time can be calming, at least in arresting the child in what he was trying to do!

Of course teachers and nursery nurses are constrained in what they *can* say and do. Physical restraint, e.g. holding the child to remove a purloined toy, is not a possibility, nor would it be likely to be effective in more than the short term. Words and actions aim to be calming and positive, but this can be difficult when youngsters consistently thwart good intentions. The best ruse is to try to anticipate the 'boiling up' and step in to change what the child is about to do, e.g. 'Jake, please come and help me to . . . ' Of course it can be difficult a) to know the right moment when there are 30 other children to keep an eye on, and you may just be keeping a weather eye on Jake, and b) because other children can resent the 'bad boy' getting jobs to do and staff may wonder if they are correct. A good strategy is to ignore the bad behaviour (if this is possible) and immediately move in to praise the child when good behaviour resumes, possibly giving the child some responsible task. In this way the good behaviour has been reinforced. Of course behaviour which may cause upset, even harm to children (even the miscreant himself), can't be ignored, and then intervention in the form of restraint needs to happen. Guidance on the form of acceptable restraint is sorely needed, especially when 'no touching' is the rule.

But of course, not all children are aggressive like Jake. Others are timid and shy, and this presents other difficulties. But why are there these differences? When does social development begin? Is nature primarily responsible or is it nurture or do both make their contribution? Fagot and Pears (1996) claim that children who have secure early attachments at home are more likely to be 'altruistic or nurturant and to create more reciprocal friendships.' Hartup (1989) however, shows that even for these fortunate children there are two kinds of primary relationships which differ in power and thus influence the kind of interaction which occurs.

Vertical relationships

Vertical relationships are those where the social power is unequal, e.g. a child with parents, teachers or nursery nurses. In these kinds of relationships the child is the receiver, the adults at home or at school act as role models who pass on social skills. It goes without saying that not all children arriving at nursery have had the same exemplars. The child who is unruly or aggressive may have had poorly socialised role models. On the other hand, children who behave badly may be using coercive behaviour – exhibiting unusual, often negative behaviour patterns to control the adult in some way. A normally calm child may scream to prevent being left (abandoned?) at nursery!

In vertical relationships, adults have responsibility for teaching and controlling behaviour. Decisions about the amount of control to use are not easy. How do parents know what to do? Many reflect on their own upbringing and copy or jettison their own childhood experiences. Others are advised by other families or local services, but of course they are dealing with an active child with a mind of his own, increasingly pushing for independence, or rejecting any offer that has been made. There are no golden rules which work for all children. Understanding the children's needs however, helps adults understand their behaviour or the tussles which can result when adults and children have different goals. The form relationships take changes as the children mature.

The summarisation given in Table 3.1 are very general cues and fluctuation between the stages is very common. Children who are less secure for whatever

Table 3.1 A developmental summary of changes in attachment patterns

Infancy	The child aims to have constant contact with the main carer(s) – the attachment figure.
Toddlerhood	Secure toddlers will allow short breaks. They may require assurance that the carer will return.
Nursery age	Greater intellectual skills and experience allow the child to spend longer times apart without anxiety.
Infant school	Children can accept 'other arrangements' as they are able to visualise, e.g. going home with another child. They recognise 'temporary' as opposed to 'permanent' arrangements.

reason (perhaps their main carer is ill, or has lost a job, or a new baby has arrived, or perhaps the home rearing practices are very different to those in nursery, causing confusion and uncertainty), may well react by being withdrawn and unco-operative, or by being noisy and aggressive in the hope of getting attention. Temporary spells of regression to an earlier stage of behaviour are very common. Understanding the cause, can help 'blips' to be dealt with patiently!

The child who uses coercive behaviour and succeeds however, begins to understand how smiles, cries or clinging on works and comes to use these behaviours deliberately. If the screaming child is taken home to television and an ice cream to quieten the sobs, the screaming has certainly been rewarded. It is likely to happen again. It is much easier to give in, for no one wants a child to be unhappy. What can be done? Calming explanations may help the child, and this is fine, or maybe the child just needs to go home and try again later? Judging genuine 'unreadiness' versus coercive behaviour is not easy.

Horizontal relationships

The other kind of relationships, i.e. horizontal ones, are peer-group friendships where cooperation and competition occur. Children create things as they play together and generally show both prosocial and antisocial behaviours, e.g. aggression. This is often caused by frustration. It can result from having wishes thwarted or sometimes by children not having the language to express what they wish to say. Those who have carers who show aggression, and in these children's eyes gain from this model of behaviour, are themselves more likely to be aggressive towards other children. However, teacher's comments like 'in the nursery we behave like this,' have to be very carefully considered to avoid alienating the parents, although everyone would hope that better ways could be transferred home. Modelling quiet and gentle ways and 'catching the child being good' are sure winners!

The development of altruism

Altruism is apparent from about three years old. Children of this age will readily show concern when another is hurt and seek to comfort by offering toys or hugs, even though their understandings of others' perceptions and feelings are still hazy. It is interesting to find that in the early years, children comfort others more than older children do (Eisenberg 1992).

How can parents and nurseries foster prosocial behaviour? Four strategies which work are:

1. Catch the child being altruistic and explain, publicly if possible, why that behaviour is pleasing. Reinforce the ways of the caring child, as well as comforting the hurt one.
2. In the nursery use opportunities to demonstrate caring behaviour and encourage the child to do so too.

Example
A new-to-nursery child sat weeping, loudly and uncontrollably, face to the wall. When other children tried to approach they were met by kicks and roars of rage. The teacher came and sat quite near the child, but avoided any contact. She picked a furry bear from the box and began to stroke it, murmuring soothing words as she did. The child gradually began to notice and the howling changed to sobbing. When the child could hear, the teacher asked, 'Could you help me please? This little bear is frightened and upset, he would like you to stroke him too.'

All this time the teacher avoided eye contact with the child – all her attention appeared to be on the bear. This was much less threatening for the child. As he gradually approached, to see what she was doing, the teacher without speaking offered the toy to the child. He took it, went back to his original place and sat stroking the toy, but as he did he began to look out into the nursery. His guard was down and he was beginning to want to play. The toy, which had given him a responsible job to do, became his favourite friend until he made friends with other children.

In this instance the teacher capitalised on the child's natural capacity for caring. By not talking directly to the child she was putting no pressure on him. Yet, by gently stroking the bear, she was demonstrating that she was a caring person. Later, when talking to the child was easier, she complimented him on how well he had tended the bear. She also made sure the other children knew how pleased she was and this counteracted the rather unfortunate start the child had had.

3. Build in opportunities for children to be helpful, e.g. let children know they are in charge of setting a snack, or arranging the musical instruments. Use badges – they are usually worn with pride! The 'naughty' ones often respond best to being given responsibilities and these can be linked to their own special interests.

4. Give lots of praise and tell the carers how well the children have done. Be positive and calm. Avoid telling the carers how naughty the children have been. They may tell you, a) it is your own fault, or that it is your job to make sure their child behaves, b) scold the child or hit out, or c) feel guilty that they have a child who behaves badly.

These negative overtures are rarely successful. The same message can be conveyed in a much more positive way, e.g. 'was there anything that caused Mary to be upset today?' conveying to the parent that unacceptable behaviour was a temporary aberration. Coping with a whole range of carers with different child rearing practices is hugely complex; it takes experience and skill to get it right!

Of course children can react in other puzzling ways. They can behave beautifully until their parent or carer appears and then throw a tantrum. Perhaps they are punishing the parent for being left even though they have been having a lovely time. One doctor explained that this was a compliment – the children were letting their tension float away with someone they could trust. Some parents find this comforting, others say it's a compliment they could do without!

The development of the gender concept

One of the most fascinating aspects of personal and social development is the child's developing sense of self. Within that, as children build pictures of themselves, comes the development of gender awareness, and recognition of the 'accepted' parameters of related behaviour which are set by different groups in society. How then do children learn their gender and sex roles? When do children develop gender-identity, i.e. recognise that they are either boys or girls? How do they know? What features do they recognise? And how do they come to understand their sex roles, i.e. the behaviours, attitudes and expectations set by society? The sex-equality flag has been flying for some time now. Are children still conditioned to feel that certain ways of behaving are appropriate for males and others for females or is this all a thing of the past?

Gender identity

Children show that they have grasped their gender identity by declaring whether they are boys or girls and by successfully naming others as such. Thomson (1975)

claims that by 15–18 months, children are identifying boys and girls correctly and using features such as hair length and clothing so to do. They can also, by age two, correctly identify their own gender by choosing a picture from a selection of boys and girls and saying 'that's like me!'

The next development is that of gender stability, i.e. the capacity to realise that the same gender endures though life. And as children learn that they are boys or girls and that they will remain so, they are also developing sex-role stereotypes. By two years, toddlers seem determined to ascribe sinks and dishes and dusters to mums and screwdrivers and ladders to dads. Similarly many children, even at two to three years, will tend to choose toys which reflect role stereotyping, i.e. girls as mums with dolls, and boys as dads with carpentry tools or cars and garages. And only slightly later, at four or five, children prefer playmates of the same sex. For all of these reasons we can claim that gender and sex-role awareness is functioning pre-school and must be considered in any study of very young children.

An interesting questions asks, 'What part do families and teachers consciously or unwittingly play in the formation of children's gender schema?' Many, even most carers, do seem to reinforce sex-typed activities by buying different toys and differently coloured clothes for boys and girls. They also give positive feedback by showing pleasure when the children play with the 'correct' toys and show 'appropriate' play behaviour. But not all parents differentiate in this way. Some are quite ambivalent about gender issues. Yet still their children develop gender bias, a favourite story being the boy who insisted all nurses were women despite having one for a dad! Why should this be?

Bigler (1995) points out that our children are immersed in a culture which is chock-a-block with gender distinctions – from designs on birthday cards to comics which emphasise prettiness as opposed to power, even aggression. School staff often say 'Good morning boys and girls', welcoming the children certainly, but still intimating that there is a difference!

Example

One farmer's daughter, the fifth in a row, was brought up hearing acquaintances say or imply, 'Still no young farmer? What a pity she wasn't a boy.' Mum's interjections, 'we only like girls in this family,' never seemed, to the child, to ring quite true and the girl was left with a feel of inadequacy, even though she did not understand why!

Of course, this was an extreme situation, the gender concept is more usually gradually assimilated – the kinds of clothes and toys, even child rearing practices all making their contribution over time. And so, given that 'significant others', i.e. parents, grandparents, teachers, nursery nurses and friends, all provide modelling and feedback about the children's developing awareness of gender, it is no wonder that by five or six they have a complex understanding of their own sex role. Having the same comprehension about the other sex doesn't develop till later, about nine or so.

There are three stages, then, in knowing one's own gender. These are

- gender concept
- gender stability
- gender constancy

Knowing one's own gender is the gender concept. Understanding that it is permanent and not dependent on hair length and type of clothes is called gender stability and is achieved by age four. However some children can be confused by the same person altering their clothes or hair length. This is quite common, even in children who have achieved stability. When they are no longer swayed by appearances, they are said to have achieved gender constancy. Children therefore know their own sex at age two or two and a half, but do not have a fully developed sense of gender until they are five or six.

Development of the sex role

Once children realise they are boys or girls, it becomes highly important to them that they behave appropriately. As soon as they have even an immature gender scheme, they fix on this 'either/or' distinction and begin to play with same sex playmates or prefer stereotyped activities (Martin and Little 1990). At age five or six the children develop a fuller understanding of 'what people like me do'. Children of this age have a strong sense of 'us' and 'them'; they develop preferences for people like themselves and have stereotyped ideas of people not like themselves. In the same way, ethnic minority children develop a strong affinity for children from their own group and at this age will actively seek out friends from their own kind. This is a stage in understanding the parameters of their own culture. The 'correct rules' are being assimilated into the children's awareness. And as they come to understand, they tend to treat the rules inflexibly, but this does decline throughout later childhood and into adolescence (Katz and Ksansnak 1994). Understanding this can help accurate assessment of the child's developing gender awareness. However, this does not mean that intolerance and prejudice can be ignored because it is likely to get less. Children must not learn to talk in terms of 'black' or 'white'.

Entrenched attitudes to ethnic differences can be displayed with pride by some early years' children and it is no easy task to provide the kind of input which will break down these attitudes without apportioning blame for the children may well be passing on comments they have heard and may not realise the hurt they convey. Heaslip (1995) advises that 'practitioners need to seek out resources, human and physical' and advocates sociodramatic play supported by sensitive interaction from the adult. The start of the twenty-first century has seen the arrival of 'Personna Dolls', i.e. dolls with the features of ethnic groups and dressed appropriately. These are proving to be a joy for many children and they are promoting a genuine interest in each other's culture.

But of course many disagreements arise from other sources. One of the most pervasive is how children address one another. Maccoby (1990) describes the different kinds of social interactions which usually occur between boys and girls and these help us to understand why friendships are formed and sustained. She called these enabling or constricting styles. Enabling styles she attributed to girls, describing the content of their interactions as:

- supportive
- expressing agreement
- making suggestions
- fostering equality

In contrast, constricting styles, typical of boys, she claimed were characterised by:

- contradicting
- interrupting
- boasting
- fostering dominance

This explains why girls' conversations tend to be longer, while boys' chats are often brief. These different styles appear at age three or four and may explain why sensitive, gentle boys prefer to play with girls. Certainly those who make assessments would find it helpful to listen in and evaluate interactions in this kind of way.

These generalisations, of course, hide the individual gender developmental patterns which cause us to puzzle over theoretical claims. Individual children may diverge markedly from the norm, their pattern being shaped by their temperament, by the child rearing practices they have experienced and by the security of their early attachments. Still, if nurseries wish to enlarge or change attitudes derived from gender bias, it is going to take much time and effort. Not only overt moves such as giving girls pictures of motor bikes instead of fairies or flowers to identify their pegs, but care with all aspects of interaction is needed so that no unspoken messages confirm what the children already suspect, i.e. that there are differences, not of their making, but possibly affecting their future.

Emotional development

The development of emotional intelligence

How do children learn to understand their own emotions and those of the people around them? How do they feel when they are hurt or angry or afraid, and how do these emotions affect their behaviour? How early can children appreciate that other people also have these feelings and how do they adjust their reactions and responses when they meet? And do these responses change in any qualitative way as the children mature? These are important questions for everyone who wishes to understand children's emotional development, because apart from its own intrinsic importance, it also impinges either positively or negatively on all other aspects of development.

There are many questions still to be answered in the field of emotional development, e.g. to find exactly how emotional trauma affects concentration and the ability to learn or how in classrooms teachers can best help children who are ill at ease, stressed or even abused. Some 'old' research has been re-tested and found to be watertight and new research has provided some answers which throw light on how children learn to understand others; so progress in this complex field is being made. Now, as much more emphasis is being placed on emotional development in curriculum guidelines, teachers will want to understand how they can best help. How does it all begin?

Interpreting facial expressions

Perhaps the most obvious answer to the question of how children learn to appreciate other peoples' feelings is through interpreting facial expressions. When does this begin? Does it have to be learned? Darwin (1872) said 'no'. He claimed that all children, almost from birth had an innate understanding of facial expressions and that they could make inferences from these and react to them, i.e. they changed their own behaviour in some way in response to their perceptions that others were happy or angry or distressed. How did he know this? He illustrated his claim by describing the reactions of his son, aged six months:

> His nurse pretended to cry, and I saw that his face instantly assumed a melancholy expression, with the corners of the mouth strongly depressed; now this child could scarcely have seen any other child crying, and never a grown-up person cry, and I doubt whether at so early an age he could have reasoned on the subject. Therefore it seems to me that an innate feeling must have told him that the pretended crying of his nurse expressed grief; and this, through the instinct of sympathy excited grief in him. (Darwin 1872)

From this kind of observation Darwin claimed that nature, not nurture, had equipped very young children to recognise expressions and understand what they meant. A linked, fascinating question, of importance to those who teach multi-ethnic groups is whether all cultures use the same expressions to show their feelings. Ekman and Friesen (1971) visited a remote part of New Guinea to find out. They observed a group who had had no contact with foreigners, who neither spoke nor understood English or Pidgin, and had seen no films (the researchers were trying to remove any environmental effects). They asked the people to listen to a story and then, from an array of photographs, to pick out faces which portrayed the emotions that had been described. They were accurate for happiness (92%), anger (84%), disgust (81%) and sadness (79%). The people were then asked to pose, showing expressions for these different emotions and when photographs were taken home, researchers here identified them correctly. This provided evidence that there were no cross cultural differences in emotional expressions (Harris 1992).

What does this mean for nursery staff? Well, they can be sure that all their children will convey their feelings using the same expressions. This takes some of the uncertainty away from planning interactions. And knowing that children can also interpret the expressions of others as they show their feelings, lets staff know that there is a sound and shared basis for explaining why certain actions fit certain situations. If a teacher knows that a child has recognised that another child is upset, then staff and children can discuss means of helping, e.g. offering comfort or giving the child privacy to recover. At nursery, children will interpret expressions at face value – not until they are six or so do children recognise that others may feel one emotion inside, and yet display another on their face!

Responding to expressions of emotions

But what about responding? It is one thing for children to understand what is going on in someone else's life, but when do they begin to respond and what kind of overtures do they make? Dunn and her colleagues (1982) asked mothers to observe and record the behaviour of their children of two to four years interacting with their younger siblings of 8 to 14 months. She found when the younger children were distressed, most of the older children comforted their brother or sister by patting or crooning and when they were hurt, the older ones made a positive move to intervene. However, when the older ones were unhappy, although most toddlers looked distressed, perhaps adopting a foetal curled up position or stamping their feet or covering their eyes, they made no move to approach or offer any solace. From pieces of research like this, it was claimed that although children from a very early age understand distress in others, not until age two or so, do they appreciate that they themselves can do something to alleviate it. In their second year children almost inevitably offered comfort to other people. This is quite a different quality of response from any that was seen in the first year of life.

Becoming a tease

This new ability to comfort doesn't develop alone. As it comes into being, children become more adept at teasing and annoying other children and adults. It is as if the two strategies come hand in hand. The important thing for teachers to realise is that children are now aware of how they can spark off either 'good' or 'bad' behaviour in others. At four years, they are also able to appreciate a causal sequence, i.e. if I do this, then this is likely to follow. These children are beginning to be able to anticipate the implications of their own behaviour on other people. And so how do they react? While many children were sorry to have caused upset, some observed children remained impassive in the face of distress, others even showed aggression. They became angry that others were upset and this made the situation worse. Observations like this cause us to ask if such aggressive children are hostile all of the time or if their attitude is context specific? If teachers can find out what is causing the anger and correct it, will all be well? Dunn and Kendrick (1982) found that although many children could be both sunny and hostile, there were children who 'responded to their siblings distress with glee, and never ever moved to comfort.'

From this research we can gather that some children learn how to inflict hurt but never learn to sympathise. Sometimes explanations of bad behaviour, e.g. 'you mustn't bite because it is really painful,' can stimulate further aggression towards the damaged child. And so no one can expect all children to develop altruism, or even with explanation, develop caring and sympathetic ways.

Developing empathy

It is reasonable to conjecture that children differ in the extent to which they can empathise with the feelings of another child and that some simply cannot appreciate another child's distress when they themselves do not feel it. They therefore cannot appreciate the perspective of another person. Different children have different levels of emotional development just as they differ intellectually or in their movement skills. But emotional development is awesome, in that failure to develop hurts others and eventually the children themselves. Some children of course have aggressive role models and may be copying patterns of behaviour they see at home. If these children have the capacity to decentre, i.e. to understand the implications of their actions for others and realise that in the longer term their peers will resent their behaviour, then perhaps they may try to change.

The capacity to understand that someone else is happy or sad or proud of some achievement brings with it an appreciation of 'why', i.e. the underlying events that have caused that emotion. If they appreciate someone else's emotion, do they feel it themselves? The answer could be 'yes' or 'no' depending on the type of event as well as the personality of the child. Think of watching a sad film. Children and adults weep when 'E.T.' goes home or when 'The Snowman' melts. They know it is just a story and yet the emotions overtake logic. The audience has empathised, felt the emotions of the characters. The filmmakers have portrayed experiences which children can relate to quite easily, and adults can remember with nostalgia – all that is required is a 'temporary suspension of disbelief in the fiction that has been created' (Harris 1992). Is this what role play in school tries to do? Is the aim to encourage a deeper understanding of other people's lives? Can children really understand what it is like to be a fireman or a nurse or is this a charade? Do they need experiences or can they imagine the characterisation in their heads? If they can't, are observers currently projecting their hopes onto what they see and being misguided by the results? This is an important question for justifying role play in the curriculum.

Understanding pretence and fantasy

Actors, dancers and teachers must often learn to portray emotions without feeling them themselves, otherwise life would be too stressful. Imagine the dancer in Martha Graham's 'Lamentations'. The dancer is in a shroud and expresses sadness and despair. Surely no one could give performances night after night feeling the depth of anguish that that role portrays?

Children too, need to be able to separate pretence from reality. Many appear to do this quite well. They don't really believe that their doll feels pain when it is dropped or that it will feel abandoned when it is left upside down on the floor. They don't believe that they become a tree when they stretch their branches to the sky. But some children blur the boundaries. Think of the child who growls like a monster then howls with fright because the monster is too real. Think of children who know that there is no one under the bed, yet leap in and cower under the covers, afraid to check. One 12-year-old was afraid to sleep because as soon as she closed her eyes she became Anne Frank and relived all the horrors that that child endured; her teacher, in giving graphic explanations to motivate some children, had not realised just how her input could affect those who had vivid imaginations. And so the answer is that many children can imagine events they have not experienced and relive, to the point of exhaustion, the emotions they portray.

Some children have a switching-off mechanism which ensures they don't sustain trauma. Children have different levels of emotional tolerance, some sensitive ones knowing full well 'It's just a story,' but suffering all the same, while others thrive on horror stories and want more and more!

The four-year-old learns to portray one emotion – probably to get attention – while actually feeling quite differently inside. I can remember standing on the pavement howling not to go to nursery and thinking, 'Why am I doing this? I like nursery.' Many children do this. They arrive at nursery appearing to be inconsolable yet the minute their parent or carer leaves, they are playing happily. Meanwhile the carer worries all morning and often has to wait and peep through the window before being convinced that the child is fine. Is this a conscious move to 'punish' the carer? Or does the child not realise the distress that has been caused?

Do children find it easier to imagine sequences of events where the characters are known or unknown? Certainly in nursery there appears to be more opportunities to play at mummies and daddies than monsters – probably because of the frightening associations or because of the anticipated noise! Yet Kuczaj (1981) tells us that imagining fantasy creatures and events in their lives can be easier for children than talking about nurses or doctors, because when they do that, they have to 'unpack what they already know, rather than starting afresh with something new.'

It is indeed difficult to understand development in all its facets. However, understanding the development of emotional intelligence is as important as the others. Perhaps its subtleties and overarching nature makes it the most important one of all.

The self-concept and self-esteem

There is no doubt that a key descriptor for the effect of social and emotional development is 'long lasting', and this can be applied to the child's self-concept or the mental image the child builds of himself as a result of interpreting his perceptions of how others view him. This picture is global in the early years and can be modified more readily than when the child is older, but nevertheless the evaluative seeds are sown as the child forms early relationships and lives through different early experiences. The child who knows he is valued, because his carers take time to listen and understand and treat him well, is likely to become a more confident, trusting youngster, one who will, in turn, listen to others and reciprocate the friendships that are offered.

The self-esteem is the name given to the part of the self-concept which deals with assessments of self-worth and judgements about the results. How is it formed? Self-esteem is the child's own picture of how well he is doing in comparison to his model of an ideal self. If the distance between the two is small, his self-esteem will be high. If the distance is great it will be low. The child himself conjures up the ideal and the characteristics of that are very important to him. If the child wants to be a good football player, as one example, being good at maths doesn't offer much consolation even if parents tell him that that is an important part of doing well at school. Another factor is that the child is more likely to accept and internalise evaluations from those that he respects. Other inputs are less valued, maybe even ignored.

The self-concept influences how children behave. If they believe they cannot do something their attitude and therefore motivation towards it is affected. A child with a high self-concept is likely to accept the challenge and be determined to succeed or shrug off the knowledge without letting it get him down. The low self-concept child, however, will see this as another insurmountable barrier and not try, 'because I can't do it anyway,' or shrug it off, but this time with aggression or despair, all negative emotions.

From these brief descriptions of complex issues, the importance of the child having many positive interactions, with lots of praise for the things he values, cannot be overstated. This is the time when the self-concept is firming up. Children must be enabled to value themselves and the contribution they can make to their social, academic, sporting and leisure groups. There are many opportunities to praise the child and encourage him to achieve the most he can.

The preschool years stand out as the critical time when social skills and personality factors interact to shape the working model of social relationships which the child creates. Between two and four, the early model is subject to revision and amendments but towards six it firms up and the patterns that exist then, tend to last through the primary years. Campbell and Pierce (1991) claim that, 'the three-, four-, or five-year-old who develops the ability to share, to read others' cues well and who learns to control aggression is likely to become a popular eight year old, whereas the hostile non-compliant child at nursery is likely to be an unpopular aggressive schoolchild.' A last word, however, must say that this is a probability statement. Many, even most of the preschool children who have difficult temperaments do not go on to develop behaviour problems though the likelihood is greater. Bates (1989) advises us to think of these children as 'vulnerable', who need love and support in greater measure than others do. If their parents and schools can offer the level of support and the caring practices that they need, these children should not go on to develop social problems. However, the children with a difficult temperament who do not have this kind of support, 'may emerge from the preschool years with serious problems in relating to others.' This is another example of the double negative – heredity and environment producing a double disadvantage.

CHAPTER 4

Perceptual-motor development

Most young children love to play outside on large apparatus or on large soft apparatus indoors. They enjoy the challenge of running faster, climbing higher, jumping onto soft mats, swinging on ropes and sliding down chutes. Many are very good at it, giving their parents and teachers heart stopping moments if they are too adventurous! Thankfully, however, most children have a built-in sense of their own skill and they stay safe. Other children, however, find moving safely on large apparatus daunting, even terrifying. Perhaps they have not had any experience of such activities; perhaps they have tried, had a fall and are reluctant to try again; perhaps they are unsure of what it is they can do; perhaps it is the bustle other children make rather than the activity itself which is off-putting; perhaps they can't

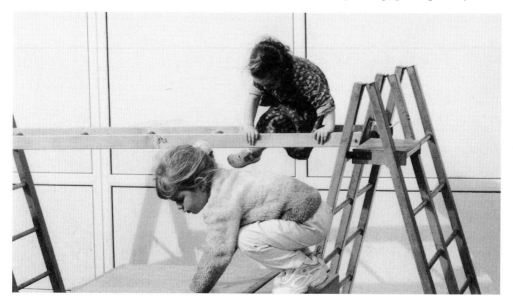

plan what they wish to do or know they just can't do it. Whatever the reason, observation of children moving needs to differentiate between the difficulties if help is to be entirely appropriate. The earlier this is done, the sooner help can be given.

The safety factor is paramount in any movement activity – safety in the provision of thick enough landing mats, in the assurance that the apparatus will not move or come apart, safety even in the distance between different pieces of apparatus so that any child falling or taking a long time to complete a turn will not be trampled on by another on a different path. This will be especially important as three-year-olds join in, as developmentally they are likely to need lower apparatus – and the older children may find it easy and tend to barge. They are also likely to need a little more time, causing the older ones to protest and hustle them and they may need more support as they try activities for the first time. It is important that teachers visualise the kinds of things the most adventurous children are likely to try so that 'accidents' caused by, e.g. children jumping from a piece of apparatus, not being able to control their speed and crashing into a wall, are avoided.

In the plan shown in Figure 4.1 there is room between the pieces of apparatus to allow any children who fall to regain their balance calmly. Different inclines house different levels of challenge so that leading-up activities are inbuilt into the plan. The layout has also been planned to allow children to show walking, running, crawling, swinging, climbing, balancing and jumping, and so it provides a sound basis for observation and assessment of the basic or fundamental movement patterns.

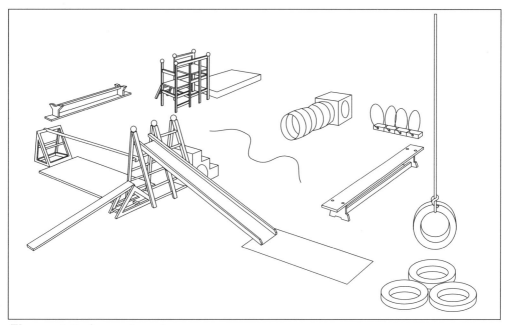

Figure 4.1 Apparatus plan

Observing movement

Having children on apparatus out-of-doors provides a wonderful opportunity to find:

- what movement patterns individual children choose to try;
- which ones they do well;
- which ones they avoid;
- what is causing them to avoid particular pieces of apparatus.

One method of observation which is particularly helpful is time sampling when the observer records exactly what the child chooses to do during a period of free choice. The level of competence can also be noted if this is appropriate by a simple tick (good) or dash (needs help) system. Figure 16 gives an example of a pie chart which one teacher used to confirm her idea that one child, Ian, was avoiding any activities which involved strength in his legs. She later used this as evidence to chase up physiotherapy help.

Even if difficulties are less severe, 'evidence' rather than 'I think' statements can be used for team planning. In Ian's case the staff devised sessions of children sitting in a circle pushing beanbags to one another with their feet – first to the person on the right, then to the left and eventually the children tried to lift the beanbag with their feet and toss it across the circle. All of this was great fun yet the activities held a good deal of leg strengthening work.

What kind of learning is movement learning?

The aim of perceptual-motor programmes in the early years and later physical education lessons in school, is that children should be able to move efficiently, effectively and safely in different environments. Some children will find everyday coping skills problematic, they will fluff even a simple movement task. Others will manage quite well and some will choose and have the ability to be sports stars. All of the children will find that being able to play football or to swim gives them credibility in the eyes of their friends and so it is very important for their self-esteem to be able to join in, and preferably to play well.

To be able to do this they need accurate:

Perception – they have to be able to interpret perceptual cues from the environment accurately.

Planning/organisational skills – they have to know what it is they wish to do, and the sequence of movements which will accomplish this. They have to be able to build a mental model.

Execution skills – they have to have the movement abilities to allow their movements to be efficient and effective.

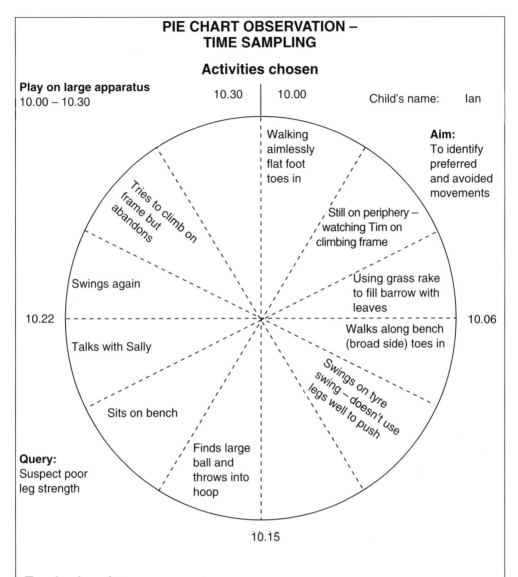

PIE CHART OBSERVATION – TIME SAMPLING

Activities chosen

Play on large apparatus
10.00 – 10.30

10.30 | 10.00

Child's name: Ian

Aim:
To identify
preferred
and avoided
movements

Walking
aimlessly
flat foot
toes in

Tries to climb on frame but abandons

Still on periphery –
watching Tim on
climbing frame

Swings again

Using grass rake
to fill barrow with
leaves

10.22

Talks with Sally

Walks along bench
(broad side) toes in

10.06

Swings on tyre
swing – doesn't use
legs well to push

Sits on bench

Query:
Suspect poor
leg strength

Finds large
ball and
throws into
hoop

10.15

Teacher's written comments:

'The pie-charts show Ian consistently avoiding running, jumping and climbing activities. This backs up my concern that he has inadequate strength in his legs.'

Action: Encourage climbing on low inclined plank and on ladder. Offer support. Check if access to physiotherapist is possible.

Figure 4.2 Pie chart time sampling

It is vitally important that observations and assessments of children's difficulties consider each aspect so that any difficulties can be pinpointed and the correct kind of help given. It can be frustrating for a child to be helped to practise the individual movements within a sequence if help is really needed with clarifying the planning, i.e. what movement follows another, or alternatively to be asked about planning when help with the technicalities of the attempted movement is the thing that is required.

The three parts can also be seen as an input-output map as shown in Figure 4.3.

When children move, they make a series of perceptual–motor decisions. These are based on the information coming from the environment through the senses and this is then interpreted in the brain. In turn this message is relayed to the muscles and joints and they are stimulated to give a movement response.

To be able to move well, without fumbling or stumbling, the perceptual input from the different senses must be accurate and the processing mechanism sound. If either inaccurate or inadequate perceptual information starts off the process, then the ensuing interpretation of the information will be flawed. If there is immaturity within the cerebral cortex, 'correct' pathways will not be reinforced and the messages will be scrambled, going perhaps to all four limbs instead of the one or two which are needed to carry out the task. This hampers efficient and precise movement. And finally, at the execution stage, the child must have the movement abilities to fulfil the instructions which are received.

The feedback loop shown in the diagram is an important part of the process which is really cyclical, not linear. This means that the imprint of the movement pattern is stored then used as a basis for further learning. This helps when a similar, more challenging movement is attempted. If the original has been poorly constructed, however, then subsequent attempts have a faulty recipe and the resulting movement patterns are impaired. This explains why practice alone will not necessarily improve performance, because unless the movement patterns are correct, the children will just get faster at doing the wrong thing.

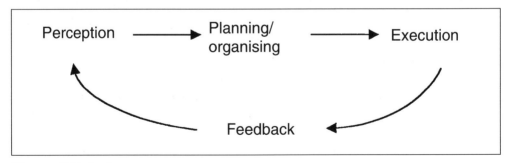

Figure 4.3 An input-output map

Planning and organisation

The second aspect of moving well comes under the heading of 'planning and organisation'. There is a subtle difference which can cause observers to make an incorrect diagnosis. Some children will not be able to build a mental model – they won't know what it is they want to do. They have a planning deficit. They can be seen wandering around looking lost. Given single, clear instructions they can manage a task quite well. What they can't do is carry out a 'do this, then that' kind of task. As they can't visualise the order of events, they are unsure of what comes next. And if they can't anticipate the outcome of movements, then they are unable to evaluate the wisdom of doing the movements at all. Safety worries are paramount for children like this. If these difficulties are combined with poor 3-D vision judgements, e.g. how deep is the water, how far away is the apparatus or even the approaching car, parents will worry when the children want to be independent. Some children, especially those with dyspraxia, can manage to complete a straightforward task, but the next day, they appear to have completely forgotten their success. This is so frustrating for the teacher and so inexplicably difficult for the children. It is easy to understand why some feel overwhelmed and totally incompetent.

Other children *can* plan, they can describe what they wish to do, but they do not have the organisational skills to carry it out. And so they do things in the wrong order, e.g. they know they have to get dressed and they can do it slowly, but they put their trousers on before pants or shoes before socks. (There is now a computer programme based on getting dressed which asks children to identify which garment goes on first.) These children would love to circuit round the apparatus, and in purely physical terms there is no reason why not, but the intellectual component, the sequence planning defeats them. They have to tackle one thing at a time and plan for that. They have to tackle each movement as a first time try even though they have attempted it before. None of their movements are automatic, each has to be thought through. This takes time and effort. Other children understandably pressing for their turn don't help. This is another reason why the apparatus needs to be well spaced with different approach runs to the higher pieces to avoid queues. These children get tired quickly because of operating at the conscious level all day. This is called ideational dyspraxia.

In school, any kind of timetabling/structure to the day is difficult for these children. Getting organised in school – finding a jotter, taking it to a desk, identifying a work card and choosing a sharp pencil – can be guided by a sympathetic teacher, but finding the way unsupervised from one room to another is really problematic. Many children with this difficulty also appear to have no sense of time and so, 'Be ready in five minutes' or any kind of 'Let's do this first and then that later' is not understood in the sequence of time sense.

Those who don't understand the children's organisational difficulties can become irritated. They 'never know where they are going,' 'are always lagging behind,' or 'are totally disorganised,' are usual, if unkind and less than helpful descriptors.

What can be done to help?

At the conceptualisation stage, talking with the children, asking, 'What is it that you would like to do?' can indicate whether the children have ideas and plans as a basis for acting. Observing the children carefully to see whether they are waiting and copying rather than following some plan of their own is a useful ploy. It is important that adults recognise the difference between the two kinds of problem because suggesting ideas to children who already know what they want to do is confusing and dispiriting if they feel constrained to jettison their own plans. Much better if teachers discover the children's plans if they have them, and then say 'Right, now let's work out how we are going to manage that,' and support the children as they try. One is helping with ideas, the other with organisational strategies to carry them out. Needless to say both should be done in a positive helpful manner using as much of the children's input as possible. One of the hardest teaching jobs is learning to listen and not take over from a slower child because this takes the joy of achievement away.

Examples
'Show me the basket that is going to catch the ball. Is it strong? Where are your elbows? In to your sides? Feel them pressing? Make sure your fingers are close together so that the ball doesn't slip through. Now you are ready. Watch the ball. Well done.'

'Let me hold your coat. Now where is your arm going to go? Can you shoot your fingers through? Can you feel them? Wiggle them if you can!'

In these kinds of learning experiences, the teachers are breaking down the tasks and doing much of the work of ordering the activity. This kind of input helps the children remember the correct sequence of events. The children are also being asked to feel where their body parts are, even when they are out of sight. This should help them develop a sense of what comes first, second, and third, and by identifying the function of the different body parts, help them become less dependent on visual cues.

Execution: carrying out the movement

Many children can move well. They are coordinated and dexterous, often challenging their competence by adding equipment such as roller blades or ballet shoes or skis – all to increase balance and speed demands. Assessing these children is straightforward – they can do it well. Unfortunately other children, as many as 8–10% (The Dyspraxia Foundation 1999) have coordination or balance difficulties which don't go away, and which make life difficult, even distressing. This emphasises the importance of assessment. Teachers need to understand exactly what is involved in moving well if these children are to be helped. How can observation of children moving be simplified? One way is by breaking down complex movements first of all by the type of movements which are done. Movements can be subdivided into three types.

These are:

1. Gross movements.
2. Fine movements.
3. Manipulative skills.

1 Gross movements

Gross movements use the large muscle groups which work together to produce actions such as walking, running, jumping and climbing. They need a good deal of strength, control and whole body coordination. These basic movement patterns develop as children mature, although even in the early years some children will be very competent. The different levels of skill which children display have been divided into 'immature, mature and sports skill patterns' by authors such as Gallahue and Ozmun (1995) and Macintyre and Arrowsmith (1988).

2 Fine movements

The demands made by fine movements are different – speaking, eating, writing and playing the piano are examples that show where only small body parts are used. These can be easier for some children because when one part of the body is 'fixed', as in sitting, it does not need to be controlled and full concentration can go to the moving parts. But of course fine movements can be very intricate, involving hand–eye coordination, e.g. cutting food, threading beads or greater rhythmical awareness, e.g. in playing the piano, or significant control in a small area, e.g. in writing or colouring in, even in speaking, and so some children find them difficult.

These movements also can involve the children in 'crossing the midline of the body' as in drawing a rainbow or reaching across to tie laces on the other foot and this is very often tricky. In fact finding difficulty in crossing the midline is one symptom of dyspraxia. Teachers need to note this difficulty carefully in any profile of needs. A related difficulty comes if children have not established hand dominance. This may not happen till children are six but it can cause the children to appear uncoordinated and clumsy as they fumble, undecided which hand to use.

In young children, gross movements involving balance and coordination of the large muscle groups are developed first. This explains why some children can run yet be unable to control a pencil, although of course children have been practising running movements longer! This sequence of development also explains why children's difficulties may not be apparent in the earliest stages. Parents can miss fine motor skill difficulties because they assume that because the gross motor skills are achieved, the others, that is the fine motor skills, will be proficient as well.

3 Manipulative skills

This kind of activity requires that children manipulate 'outside objects' such as pencils or bats, knives and forks. To do this they have to cope with added control demands, e.g. holding the swinging bat against the impact of the ball. They also have to have a developed sense of body boundary, i.e. where they end and the object begins. And of course they have to make the object follow a pattern as in writing or a trajectory when throwing a ball. This takes practice and can be very difficult if muscle tone is poor. Children with poor shoulder control will find it

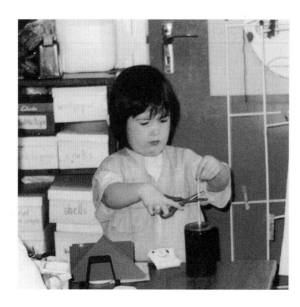

difficult to control a pencil, especially if they are not sitting at the correct height of table. Having a triangular grip can help children whose pincer grip is not well developed.

Analysing movement patterns

Every movement, large or small, has three parts i.e. preparation, action and recovery (see Figure 4.4). When movement is smooth and efficient, the three parts flow together and the momentum from one part carries on to help the next. In sequential movements, the recovery from the first completed movement blends with the preparation for the second.

In efficient movement, the preparatory phase 'gets the body ready' by deciding on the speed that will be needed, the direction of travel, the parts of the body to be used and the sequence of the action. Complex movement patterns require a great deal of mental planning and preparation. Think of attempting a long jump or even the triple jump! All of the stride pattern and timing elements have to be rehearsed before the athletes begin. This is why they take some time contemplating all the demands of the task before setting off. Children attempting tasks such as running and jumping off a bench have the added difficulty of watching others to ensure that they will not run across their path and spoil their attempt. Children who can't plan ahead, i.e. those who can't visualise what comes next, will have to make on-the-spot decisions and if they are flustered by being rushed they may well be the wrong ones. Similarly, children who can't cut out visual distractors have difficulties because movements, e.g. other children running by, cause them to look up and make them lose their concentration. Lots of children need more time, more help and possibly less challenge if they are to stay safe. The demands of the environment need to be reduced to allow them to be successful. Normally, with experience, i.e. when movements become habitual, planning does become easier, even automatic. Then movements are carried out with minimum effort, they are efficient.

The underlying motor or movement abilities which allow effective and efficient movements to happen are 'balance', 'control' and 'coordination'. During the action, strength is needed, enough momentum to suit the type of action and balance, i.e. both dynamic balance to aid control during movement and static balance to allow movement to come to a stop. At the end, there will be a release of strength so that the

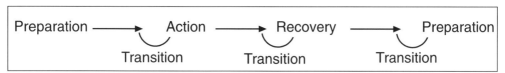

Figure 4.4 Analysis of a movement pattern

recovery can be resilient, leading smoothly into the next preparation. The recovery must also sustain the balance and control so that it doesn't throw the next action awry.

Flowing movement has an in-built rhythm and recognising this can clarify the pattern, e.g. where the strong parts need to come, and so help the pattern to be done well. Children can be helped to 'listen' for the rhythm, then clap or stamp it out. This is very good for children who have difficulty listening as it helps them visualise a successful movement pattern.

It can be quite difficult for observers to distinguish between the three phases of a movement, especially if it is done quickly. And sometimes the difficulty lies in the transitions, i.e. the links between each part when adjustments have to be made. These involve kinesthetically anticipating the next part of the action and reacting to the demands of the movement and the environment, usually quickly! Perhaps the children need to realise that they have to get their feet ready to change direction or if, e.g., they have done a forward roll and want to get back to their feet, they have to retain a rounded shape to keep the momentum going rather than flattening out and finishing the action lying on the ground.

As the actual patterns are carried out, the children are making decisions about:

- the speed of the movement, i.e. very quick – quick – medium pace – slow – very slow,
- the strength of the movement, i.e.very strong – medium strength – delicate, fine,
- the space the movement needs – wide – narrow – direct – flexible,
- the direction of the movement, i.e. forwards – backwards – diagonally – in a curve – zig-zag,
- the flow of the movement, i.e. tightly held – jerky – smooth – free flowing,

and these movement factors should be analysed by the observers too.

The wrong selection is likely to be be clearly demonstrated if you think of a three- to five-year-old trying to throw a ball. The first thing is that the stance is likely to show that the leading foot is on the same side as the throwing arm. This means that there can be no turn of the body and no propulsion by the throwing arm and so the throw stays as a 'poke'. The wrong preparation influences the 'action' because the stance leaves no room for the arm to swing back, and so the elbow leads into the throw. But hardest of all for young children is the moment of releasing the ball. They use too much strength to grip, their fingers are curled tightly round the ball, the hand opens too late and the ball dribbles down to land at their feet. You can see that if the first part of the action sequence is faulty, the whole action falls apart. Of course the teacher must know the component parts of an effective throw so that the diagnosis can be accurate and the remediation helpful.

The perceptual abilities which are key movement abilities also need to be understood and assessed if teachers are to help movement, just as they help other competences such as language development or social skills. They are:

Body awareness
Spatial awareness
Rhythmic awareness
Balance
Coordination
Speed of movement

Body awareness

Some children have very little awareness of their bodies as they move. They do not realise the effect which moving one part of their body has on other parts. They find it difficult to move one part by itself and they are confused about where their own bodies end and the outside world begins. Very young children do use whole-body movements for any task but generally, as they grow older, these gross movements should become refined and the action more deft. For example, picking up an object develops from the baby's whole hand grab to finger–thumb precision. Another difficulty which children with poor body awareness have is in knowing how far one body part is from the other. If children don't have a clear idea of this, then movements like tying laces or lifting a bucket of sand are clumsy and awkward. It affects any actions where moving two hands together is necessary. If children also misjudge distances, e.g. how far the football is from their kicking foot, then they are likely to overrun the ball or apply maximum force too soon and the action is ineffective.

Spatial awareness

This refers to the children's understanding of where the different parts of their bodies are in space and of the relationship of these parts to each other and to objects. Children who bump into things or who constantly trip and fall may have poor spatial awareness. They fumble when trying to catch a ball, either because they have not stretched to the right place or because they have not been able to follow the trajectory of the flight. Their hands are not ready in time. Feet trip up on stairs or climbing apparatus because the height is not estimated correctly.

Balance may be difficult for children who do not appreciate where arms should be in space to help them keep upright. Older children might appear even more clumsy when they are working on a complex movement sequence in the gym or when they are attempting to cooperate in games or dance because movements such as turning involve ever-changing cues from the environment.

Spatial awareness can be developed by providing lots of simple learning experiences which encourage the pupil to make spatial judgements, e.g. 'stand near/far away from your partner', or passing the parcel type games which involve stretching grasping, then letting go. Children need plenty of opportunities to practise, and simple everyday tasks can be helpful and just as successful as specific exercises designed to promote the kind of learning that is required, so everyone can help.

Rhythmic awareness

Every movement has a preparation phase, an action phase and a recovery phase. When these three phases blend together so that recovery leads into preparation which leads into the action, a rhythm emerges. A break in the rhythm probably means that the action is inefficient. It can be very helpful for teachers to clap out the rhythm of actions and in this way ensure that the children are able to hear it. Listening and clapping out the rhythm together is fun; it promotes body and spatial awareness and it feeds into the children knowing where to apply strength or where to move quickly.

Maintaining a 'gross' movement rhythm, e.g. in skipping, is quite a different ability from the fine rhythm demonstrated in clapping a beat or playing the piano. In these kinds of movements the large muscle groups must be controlled, and strength must be gathered and released at the appropriate times. And so, even if children can demonstrate fine motor skills rhythmically, the adults cannot assume that their gross movement rhythm is sound. The alternative is also true. Older primary children can be helped to greater awareness by listening to the *sound* of their movement patterns. Feet make a most satisfactory noise on the wooden floor and the even stride of a running pattern can be contrasted with that used in dodging and marking. The sound matches the size of the stride pattern. The successful dodge will probably have one long stride followed by a rapid fire of short ones. The noise tells if the first stride was definite enough to pull the marker away and if the short strides were fast enough to allow the dodger to escape.

The noise of a shuttlecock on a wooden bat can help build a rally as the amount of strength required can be gauged from the sound as well as the trajectory of the flight. The rhythm also helps spatial judgments – the quick pattern of short hits contrasting most satisfactorily with the smash of the longer shot.

Intrinsic rhythm
The rhythm within a movement phrase need not be determined by actions such as skipping or hitting a ball to a partner. The freedom within expressive movement means that a rhythm can emerge as a dance or drama sequence is composed. No

external rhythm need be imposed as is the case when music or poetry acts as a stimulus – the intrinsic rhythm can come from the type of movement chosen and develop as children work together to compose a dance phrase. Once this rhythm is internalised, it can be practised as in any other activity.

The two girls in the picture are composing a dance based on their selection of action words. They are showing their interpretation of 'dashing together, swirling round, then gently sinking to the floor.' As they show the qualities of the words through their expressive movement, their own rhythmic pattern emerges and soon they are able to say the action words as they dance.

Expressive movement helps the development of gross motor skills when sequences include the basic movement patterns. If they are given their expressive names, then as children experience the different qualities within the movements, their vocabulary develops too.

Expressive movement patterns
Walking becomes – creeping or sauntering or prowling or stalking, etc.

Running becomes – dashing or darting or rushing or zipping etc.

Jumping becomes – bounding or exploding or popping or leaping, etc.

Gesturing becomes – pointing or beckoning or turning or twisting or crumpling or stretching or sinking or growing, i.e. any action which happens 'on the spot'.

Being still becomes – freezing or holding or waiting or pausing.

If the teacher or the children themselves select one word from each type of action, they can be ordered into an expressive movement phrase. One example could be:

Dash and freeze, crumple and pop pop pop!

Analysing the expressive content of that phrase shows that contrasts in speed and distance are built in and movements on the spot give the children time to 'get ready' for the next action phrase.

Dash – moving quickly and lightly, skimming the floor for a short distance (to retain the quality of the action).

Freeze – stopping suddenly with control - in a high position because of the next action.

Crumple – sinking slowly with either a rounded or jagged action. Gathering strength – on feet ready to

Pop – exploding quickly, arms moving out from the centre of the body. Popping out to the original position ready to begin again. This might use three or four 'pops' depending on the available space.

The dance can be built into a duo with the children coming together and apart so that they develop an awareness of someone else's movement and adjust their timing and use of space. From duos, fours can come together to use the practised components and revamp their use of space and so compose a group dance, perhaps doing parts together or with some in sequence. Again awareness of other children, memorising the short dance and retaining the quality of the chosen movements provides an enjoyable challenge.

The children should be encouraged to select actions which allow them to show contrasts for these blend easily and very satisfyingly into a rhythmical dance. Some other examples could be:

Swirl and hold, swirl and hold, creep away, creep away, pounce and freeze.

In this kind of phrase, words are repeated to give time for the intrinsic rhythm to be felt. If some children find swirling difficult, they can take quite a time on the 'hold' so that their balance is reestablished ready for the next phrase.

To give the dancers more travelling space, the group can be subdivided and then the children who are watching try to guess the words the dancers are demonstrating, or some try to accompany the dance with percussion (not the music makers providing the stimulus for the dance because this would be another kind of experience where the rhythm was imposed). If this happens, then everyone is able to participate and learning words comes naturally alongside learning about the dance. Once more learning is part of a play scenario.

In this type of activity there are no 'outside' things to control and so children who have difficulties can join in and enjoy their movement lesson too.

Dance drama
Once more qualitative words are understood, acting out parts of stories can be fun, e.g. 'The giant stomped into the castle', 'The tigers prowled through the long grass,' 'The lightning flashed across the sky', or 'The smoke swirled from the bonfire'. The list is endless and after 'moving the words' the children should understand their meaning and where they might be applied, and hopefully they will retain some to use in their storytelling or imaginative writing!

Balance

The most significant ability in movement is balance, as it affects almost everything that the child is required to do. Some authors call balance 'postural control' and indeed this term does suggest a more dynamic demonstration of the ability, for balance is not just the ability to stand securely on one leg for a few minutes: it sustains the position of the body in the air in a jump, it steadies the body during a throwing action and it helps body control during changes of direction. If adults suspect that a child's balance is faulty, then they must observe the child moving and being still, i.e. assessing both static and dynamic (or moving) balance.

Vision helps considerably in the maintenance of balance and if the child experiences difficulties, help in using visual cues may provide valuable compensation. Children can be encouraged to fix their eyes on a particular spot on the wall, and in so doing, they gain a stable point of reference. Then they can align their position with that spot. Mirrors are sometimes used to help children with this difficulty, though their 'back to front' cues can be confusing. Children need time to be steady, to look, to *feel* the correct alignment and then to try the movement over and over again.

Coordination

Coordination is the ability to control the independent body parts involved in a complex movement pattern and to integrate these parts in a single smooth successful effort to achieve some goal. The type needed varies according to the complexity and nature of the task. It differs according to how many body parts are involved in the movement and each task requires that the appropriate body parts must be sequenced in a particular way and in a particular time-pattern. A specific skill may involve one kind of coordination, e.g. eye–foot coordination as in kicking a ball or hand–eye as in throwing an object towards a target, or overall body coordination such as is needed in a gymnastic or dance sequence. Skill in one form of coordination does not necessarily indicate skill in another, so challenges involving a variety of coordination skills are necessary to ensure that all of the underlying abilities are developed.

Sometimes young children can be helped if they have one part of their body 'fixed', i.e. they can try an action while sitting first, just to get the feel of it. Obviously this saves them controlling their legs and feet. One example could be two children kneeling on the floor rolling a ball to one another. This could help them practise releasing the ball at the correct time, the most difficult part of the action, and also help them to feel the sweeping action of the arm, a good preparation for bowling!

Speed of movement

This refers to the time taken to react to a stimulus and to move at a chosen and appropriate speed.

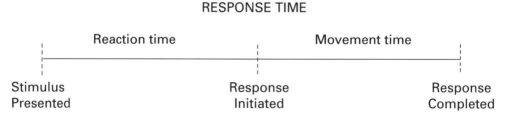

Figure 4.5 Response time

- Reaction Time* is the term used to describe the time between the perception of a given stimulus and the beginning of the response. Children with quick reaction time tend to do well in competitive activities of short duration, e.g. sprinting, net play in badminton, or in games where instructions are called out and the pupils are required to make an immediate response.
- Movement Time is the time the action takes from beginning to completion.
- Response Time (RT + MT) covers both reaction and movement time.

Reaction time should not to be confused with reflex action, which is purely automatic.

In analysing a poorly carried out action, it is important to keep the two 'times' in mind. Again, poor performance in one does not necessarily indicate poor performance in the other. Reaction time can be improved by focusing the child's attention firmly on the stimulus and perhaps giving prior warning of any sudden response, e.g. fixing eye contact with the child as you say, 'Are you ready' at the start of a race. Improving the movement time requires analysis of the movement pattern into its preparatory, action and recovery stages, so that appropriate correction may be made as necessary.

To summarise these details, a checklist is now given (see Figure 4.6). This is to facilitate recording while observing the children as they practise and become ever more effective and efficient movers and hopefully more confident youngsters. For children who are consistently clumsy or functioning at a level below that of their peers, specific tests to measure their ability in balance, coordination, speed of movement, body awareness, spatial and rhythmic awareness, may be needed. These tests, which are fun to do, have been specifically designed to isolate the faulty component so that effective remediation can be planned (see Henderson and Sugdon (1992) in Bibliography).

The checklist provides objective evidence of observed difficulty. This is a useful record to discuss with other concerned adults or to show specialists in the field of movement remediation. A more detailed movement record is in Appendix 1 (pp. 108–111).

Name of Activity . . . .

Yes   No

1. Can the child do it?   ☐   ☐

If no,

2. Check   a) Does the child understand the instructions?
b) Is the level of demand realistic?
c) Is the equipment suitable?
d) Are distractions minimised?
e) Is the child motivated to try?

If a difficulty persists,

3. Identify the movement patterns used.

Please tick   Please tick

Walking   ☐   Climbing   ☐

Running   ☐   Balancing   ☐

Crawling   ☐   Twisting   ☐

Swinging   ☐   Spinning   ☐

Turning   ☐   Throwing   ☐

Stretching   ☐   Catching   ☐

Jumping   ☐   Kicking   ☐

Hopping   ☐   Aiming   ☐

Being still   ☐

Yes   No

Study the preparation, action and recovery phases. Is one faulty?   ☐   ☐

If no

Yes   No

4. Is it the transition causing the problem?   ☐   ☐

Please tick

What is the main difficulty?   Changing speed   ☐
Changing direction   ☐
Overbalancing   ☐
Fumbling with feet   ☐
Other? If so what   _____

5. Is there a general lack of any underlying movement ability?

Please tick

Body Awareness   ☐
Spatial Awareness   ☐
Rhythmic Awareness   ☐
Balance   ☐
Co-ordination   ☐
Speed of Movement   ☐

Yes   No

6. Is the child improving with practice?   ☐   ☐

Figure 4.6 Observing children's movement patterns

CHAPTER 5

Intellectual development in the early years

In infancy and throughout the preschool years, children's brains develop rapidly, adding large numbers of dendrites and synapses and then pruning the extraneous ones. The myelination (the process of material coating the axons) of the neurons has begun, but in the motor and sensory areas it is not complete until about age six. This is why children are often rather clumsy and uncoordinated before this and explains why teachers do not wish to label children as having specific difficulties, e.g. dyspraxia, before that time – even though they know the benefits of very early intervention. They are hoping that maturation plus their own planned input will alleviate their difficulties.

Another development in the brain which begins before birth and continues through the preschool years is the specialised function of each hemisphere. The left hemisphere, which controls sensory input from the right side of the body and the movements it makes, also processes language, while the right hemisphere, which controls the left side of the body, deals with spatial information. The right side uses visual or auditory information while the left side uses words. And so different parts of the brain have different jobs to do. These become more fixed over the preschool years. Nursery staff will associate the development of hand dominance with this. Young children use either hand, only developing a strong preference for left or right from the age of three onwards. Some children, however, continue to use both hands beyond the age of six. They may be ambidextrous, but they could well be changing hands to avoid carrying out actions which require them to cross the midline of the body. Nursery staff can make useful observations and assessments here, perhaps as the children try to draw a circle, the indecisiveness in which hand to use and the avoidance of crossing the midline could indicate symptoms of dyspraxia (Dighe and Kettles 1996).

Most children (85%) turn out to be right handed and use that hand for writing and most coping skills. For these children, the left side of the brain controls both movement and language. It is interesting to find that left-handed children have less hemispheric dominance than right-handed children. They can use either hand more easily than can their right-handed friends, and as both halves of their brain are involved in more types of activity, they recover from brain injury more easily. They are also better at tasks needing spatial decisions and at some complicated mathematical tasks. Tennis stars certainly seem to benefit from being left handed. This could well be due to their ability to make fast and accurate spatial decisions, e.g. where to place the ball. However, there is a downside to being left handed too. These children are more likely to have migraine, allergies and articulation problems and suffer from ADHD (attention deficit hyperactivity disorder) (Gerschwind and Galaburda 1987).

In nurseries and schools, staff ensure that left-handed children have the correct equipment, e.g. left-handed scissors. A right-handed teacher, however, can have great difficulty demonstrating a skill to a left-handed pupil, e.g. teaching knitting! This is probably best left to a left-handed teacher; when left-handed children

observe a right-handed teacher, they need much more time to copy as they have to turn the pattern around to suit their way. But there is no need to encourage a child to change a preferred hand. Again observation and assessment is enriched by understanding the basis of individual differences, then explanations of why things are as they are, rather than only descriptions, may be made.

The development of language

The child at two and a half has a vocabulary of about 600 words. By five or six that has increased to 15,000 words – children learn ten new words each day (Pinker 1994). By three, most children can form sentences and hold conversations. This enables them to cope at nursery, e.g. in making their needs known by being able to talk with staff and other children as they play. At the same time as they have this language explosion, they develop another intellectual or cognitive tool. They can now categorise objects with similar characteristics into groups and this helps them to understand their properties. They can use this new understanding to collect similar items together, e.g in the nursery shop.

Private speech

Everyone laughs at the idea of 'having an argument with yourself and losing it', but in effect the idea of private speech originates with two- or three-year-olds who give themselves instructions as they play, e.g. 'Don't put that car there, oh no!' They also play with words, making their own rhymes and chortling as they do. Sometimes other children will take up the chant and this develops into a game (is this the thinking behind adverts such as 'utterly butterly'?). Even if the rhymes don't make much sense, they are enjoyed for the sound, rather than the meaning of the words. These play experiences can help articulation, a developing sense of rhyme and rhythm and an appreciation that language has many combinations of sounds. Like all play it is fun, especially if someone else joins in. It can be transient, no one will will mind if it stops and so there is no possibility of failure.

By age nine or so this 'private speech' has largely disappeared, but it emerges again later when complicated instructions or lists of numbers have to be memorised. Increasingly towards old age, the murmuring and muttering of early childhood happens again.

What do children gain from private speech? Children use strategies like this to monitor their own behaviour. It helps them plan, even to stay safe if they focus on one particular situation at a time.

Listening to young children use increasingly complex language alerts listeners to the pace of learning that has occurred and prompts further questions, e.g. How do they learn to speak so well? Are they simply repeating what they hear? Are they then learning by imitation? Imitation certainly plays a part, as children can be heard repeating phrases in the intonation and accent their parents use. But imitation alone cannot explain the creativeness of children's language. How do they learn to combine words and phrases in original ways?

The environment, i.e. nurture, plays a significant role in children's developing language. Adults who speak to their children about aspects of their day, read to them regularly and use a wide vocabulary themselves, are ensuring that their children will develop large vocabularies, even learn to read more easily (Snow 1997). Similarly reading stories to children in nursery gives them a good start. Snow claims that children denied language experiences at age four face 'a gap which only widens over the school years.' To try to counteract this, staff in play groups and nurseries often plan to interact more with children who have missed out, i.e. who have had little experience of being 'talked with' as opposed to 'at'. Unfortunately, this is more difficult than it sounds. Taking children from where they are by gradually extending their learning, requires skill and perseverance and ideally lots of information about the children's backgrounds. This requires the teachers to decentre, i.e. to understand their perspective derived from their upbringing, their interests and all the previous experiences they have had. The staff also need to estimate the children's 'zone of proximal development' (ZPD) (Vygotsky 1978). By appreciating where children are in terms of their learning state and their ZPD, i.e. where they are likely to be able to go when they have support, input can be planned to have the optimum effect.

But how does this occur? At the start of a task, children may have little notion of what is going to happen so teachers offer simple instructions to set the children off on the right lines. Gradually as the children recognise the aim of the task and see the purpose of their actions, i.e. as they become more competent, the teachers can withdraw direct support and give encouragement only. Gradually the 'scaffolding' (Bruner's term for support) is removed and the children are left with the satisfaction of a job well done. Similarly the task may be initiated by the children who may take it so far and then run short on ideas or motivation to complete it. Those who offer support have to understand the children's purpose, i.e. what they were attempting to achieve, and then make suggestions or offer resources to take the children over this mental block. Vygotsky was anxious that children had this support. He saw unaided problem solving as only utilising what cognitive functioning the child already had mastered. He claimed that progress was dependent on children having the correct kind and amount of assistance at the right time.

Conversations: how teachers can best help children to communicate

One of the most interesting aspects of language development is how young children learn to communicate with their peers (pragmatics) and how they change their behaviour and adapt their speech to the listener. This can be spotted in two-year-olds and increases with age until playground language can almost make children sound bilingual! To do this successfully, children have to anticipate how their listeners will respond and make their own communications fit this scene, be it at home, playing outside, in the playground, wherever. Some children coming to nursery will have to make vast changes in their usual mode of interaction and may take some time to assimilate all the nuances of an acceptable mode. On the other hand, children with articulation difficulties are often understood by the other children when adults are at a loss to know what they are saying.

If this support concerns helping children's communication skills, it is best if those who offer it can avoid asking the children closed questions, i.e. the kind which only require a one word answer, for these effectively shut down any chance of long conversations.

In a PhD study, Bryson (2000) worked with student teachers who wished to improve their interaction skills with children in the nursery. The students had explained that when they tried to talk with the children, they resorted to questions, 'just to have something to say', e.g. 'What is your name?', 'What do you like to play with?', 'Do you come to nursery very day?', or even worse 'What's that?' when 'what that was' was perfectly obvious to the children! In these cases, the children's answers were monosyllabic and sometimes scornful. Very often the children just ignored the students' interventions and walked away. Bryson, an experienced nursery head teacher herself, provided a list of interaction strategies for the students which she envisaged would be helpful. These were:

- to use phatics (mmm? Oh? Tell me more, go on . . .) i.e. encouraging noises or very brief inputs which do not break the flow of the children's thoughts;
- to tell the children something from their own experience which they could share, e.g. 'I remember being at the seaside . . .', or simply
- to wait in companionable silence till the child was ready to continue.

Whenever possible, however, the best strategy was:

- to let the children initiate the conversation and follow their agenda.

While the students reported that knowing the strategies was helpful in trying to plan ahead, some found trying to recall the list in the midst of initiating conversations inhibiting. Later, reflecting on their attempts, they explained that conversations only became natural and easier when they got to know the children, their interests and aptitudes. Then, in the light of this understanding, they could estimate their ZPD. The students had been driven to early interactions with the children by the unwritten and quite false supposition that because they were practising teachers, they had to justify their presence; they had to get in there and talk! Once they knew they could wait until they had observed the children at play and had something real to talk about, everyone had a much more productive and happier time.

This kind of interaction is also very important in reading stories and then finding what the children have understood, what information they have retained or indeed how they have been able to think logically about the train of events in the story and make appropriate suggestions as to how it might continue. One way of achieving this is through dialogic reading. In this strategy the parents or teachers who are reading pause in the story and pose problems, e.g. 'However will that little bear get home?' or 'What do you think will happen now?' Or 'Snow White has found this house in the woods. She is tired and hungry. What do you think she'll do?' The point is that although the answers could seem rhetorical to us, who know the original stories, there are possibilities for alternatives and children can be imaginative and thoughtful in giving responses. This helps in developing their imaginative writing skills as well as boosting their confidence when their suggestions form part of the final story. Crain-Thoreson and Dale (1995) found that when children with language delay were read to in this special way, i.e. with dialogic reading, their language skills significantly improved.

Learning stages

One question which is important to all those involved in planning children's education is whether or not there are learning stages, i.e. are the children only equipped to learn certain kinds of things at certain times and are these age related? Further important questions ask, 'Are these differences long lasting or do they change over time without teaching and if they do, is intervention really necessary?'. Certainly observations of children at play show that they progress through differ- ent kinds of play as they mature – e.g. moving from solitary play, through parallel play to preferring cooperative play with friends. This would suggest that development itself involves fundamental change. But is that change quantitive, i.e. do children use more of the same kind of learning strategies and coping skills, or is it qualitative, are there significant conceptual changes in the way children learn? If there are, the stages of learning theory would be endorsed and all those concerned with educating children would need to know what these changes involved, e.g. what learning abilities had developed at what age. However, if there are no learning stages but only additions to a body of knowledge, then the process of learning would not need to be planned according to stage theory.

Certainly much everyday language would endorse the concept of stages, e.g. the 'terrible twos', with parents comforted by the notion that this is a passing phase and everyone will survive. Colic at three months, rebellion at adolescence, infirmity at old age, are these also stages with their own characteristics? There are certainly times when behaviour is very different. However, stage theory goes beyond this to suggest that there are new understandings and competences at each stage which make it possible for children to learn new things.

Children's drawings provide a good example (see Figure 5.1). After a dressing up in older fashioned clothes session, this drawing was done by Catriona aged six. Although it is quite sophisticated in that the mother's shoulders turn to match the head (in the poke bonnet), the child draws the pram wheels in this strange position because she knows they are there. Older children would draw only what they 'see'.

The best-known stage test is Piaget's work on conservation (Piaget and Inhelder 1969). He demonstrated that children needed a certain level of comprehension and reasoning if they were to make accurate judgments, e.g. to recognise that the same amount of liquid poured into differently shaped glasses does not alter because the shape of the glass makes it look as if it does. He claimed that children would not be able to conserve, i.e. recognise the stability of the amount of water, to distinguish between appearance and

Figure 5.1 Lady with pram

'reality', before six or seven. There are significant implications for teaching here. Should teachers wait until the children's competences develop naturally or should they 'teach', i.e. give explanations to hurry the child along? And if they do this, can the skills and abilities, which depend on conceptual understanding, be developed faster in any meaningful way? Or does this add unnecessary stress or encourage the children to use rote learning rather than developing their understanding? Those who support stage theory claim that it provides a clear structure for planning the kind of learning experiences which are most appropriate at different ages.

Other theorists, however, claim that stages are artificial and that planning in this way could hinder some children's learning. Donaldson and Hughes (Donaldson 1979) revamped Piaget's tests using child-friendly language and found that children could grasp and explain the concepts much earlier. The important outcomes from this research were that teachers should not underestimate what children can do. If learning is phrased in familiar terms and is developed from the child's own experiences, they will be enabled to cope. And so this kind of finding would seem to work against the concept of stages. The whole idea is one which is still open to debate.

Certainly these deliberations house fundamental considerations for those who develop learning through play. They highlight the timing of introducing more formal teaching and more complex play activities, and they show how important it is to analyse the demands which different learning activities make, in relation to the developmental profile of the children in their care.

Children and intelligence

As everyone knows, children differ in their aptitudes, their abilities, their interests and in their motivation to do different things. Some find learning easy, others struggle to learn, some are motivated to keep learning in the academic sense while others prefer to do other, more practical things. However, those who do well at school are usually considered to be 'intelligent', especially if they do well across the curriculum. If they do, then this would seem to agree with those who claim that there is one kind of intelligence, a general factor, 'g', which permeates across learning and doing. This means that children have the capacity for similar levels of achievement across the board. However, through analysing exactly what high achievers were accomplishing, and considering all the various kinds of problems they were solving, researchers such as Gardner (1983) argued that there were 'at least six different kinds of intelligence.' These he called 'frames of mind':

Linguistic intelligence   seen in those who use language fluently, or in a novel and appropriate way; in those who explain clearly or argue convincingly; in those who use language in an original, descriptive mode, such as poetry.

Musical intelligence   seen in those who are particularly sensitive to rhythm and pitch. This is often expressed in the ability to sing well or play an instrument but may be housed in those who appreciate music in an analytic, considered way.

Logical mathematical intelligence   seen in those who remember facts, score well on tests which demand quick recall; in those who can apply known facts to new situations, i.e. transfer learning appropriately; in those who have organisational/planning skills. Mathematicians and scientists have this kind of intelligence.

Spatial intelligence   seen in those who can visualise complex designs from different perspectives such as architects or graphic artists; those who can appreciate spatial moves, e.g. on a chess board, snooker table or sports field.

Bodily kinesthetic intelligence   seen in those with accurate visual and kinesthetic perception; in those who require to balance precariously such as ballet dancers or tree surgeons; in those who use non-verbal behaviour to convey messages, e.g. mime artists or impressionists.

Personal intelligence seen in those who can interpret their own feelings accurately, and those who can interpret the feelings, moods, temperaments of others.

This last mode overlaps with Sternberg's (1985) contextual intelligence. He develops Gardener's idea by talking of those who use their perception of others to manipulate their social setting. They tune in and then make the most of the situation, e.g. the child who consciously behaves in a way which will gain him praise or some other kind of reward. Often people talk of 'street wise children'. They are demonstrating contextual intelligence!

Gardner's (1983) 'frames of mind' fit well with the division of development into its social and emotional, perceptual motor and intellectual aspects. In putting forward this differentiation, Gardner is supporting the curricular plan which from age three, advocates a wide experience of learning activities so that each mode of intelligence may have the opportunity to flourish.

Intelligence quotient

IQ tests were originally designed to be culture and experience free so that they measured innate potential without any environmental effect. They tried to measure the range of skills which indicated likely success in schools 'and they do this quite well for a limited number of topics' (Bee 1995). What they don't do, is cover competences like creative or original thinking, e.g. the ability to find a novel solution to a problem, or social skills, e.g. the ability to adjust to fit into a group, or movement skills, e.g. the ability to adjust one's movement to suit a changing terrain, all aspects covered by Gardner (1983) in his 'frames of mind' model of intelligence.

An IQ test is a very specific tool, useful to identify differences in children at any one time, but its limitations must be recognised, for even the stress of having a test could surely alter the score. This, of course, could be exacerbated by parents. If they see the test as a measure which will determine their child's success in life, they may well pass on anxieties about 'doing well' to their children, and unwittingly cause them to 'freeze'. Some may buy test books and attempt to teach the test. Perhaps this explains why many authorities no longer use them. If the environment in the shape of parents or teachers could make a difference to the score, is the test valid? Is it still culture and experience free?

Influences on intelligence

Once again, to try to explain intelligence, we need to confront the nature/nurture issue. Is intellectual capacity inherited and therefore largely fixed or is it amenable to change and if so what part does the environment play?

Heredity

Many psychologists who believe IQ is inherited, base much of their evidence on twin studies. Brody (1992) studied identical twins reared together, in the same environment, and found the scores of their intelligence correlated at .85, a very high score. Identical twins reared apart, and so subject to different environmental influences, still showed a high score, between .60 and .70 in different studies. These high correlations indicate a strong genetic component. Similarly, studies of adopted children show that their IQ is nearer that of their birth parents than that of their adoptive ones. This would also support the nature/heredity/genetic stance.

Environment

What of the other camp then? What part does environment play? It is tremendously difficult to control factors in different groups of children so that findings can be generalised in any meaningful way. Capron and Duyme (1989) tried to do this by carrying out an extensive study which included children from all the social strata – from highly advantaged to severely disadvantaged families and from parents with high IQs to those with much lower scores. He found that there was a difference of 11 or 12 points for children reared in advantaged homes. This meant that environmental support could influence IQ.

World-wide studies now apportion 50% of the variation in IQ scores to heredity and the rest to environmental influence or the interaction of heredity and environment together. And so genes indicate a range of possible functioning, i.e. they give upper and lower boundaries, but the environment can significantly influence where, within that range, children can function. And so all early years carers, while not being able to produce a genius in every child, can give their children a boost so that they reach their potential. This means that although there may not be a large IQ change, their children will be better able to play the fullest role that they can, both in school and at home.

CHAPTER 6

Understanding children who find it difficult to play

One of the saddest things is to hear children say, 'no one will let me play,' and parents and nursery staff often feel helpless and inadequate in the face of their children's distress. Sometimes adults understand what is wrong because their children have recognised difficulties such as autism which makes interacting very difficult, but very often there is no apparent (to adults that is) reason why some children don't get to play. Adults know that this is terrible for the children at this moment in time and they fear that any lasting exclusion may negatively affect their developing self-esteem. If this happens, the children may begin to believe they are different, less valued in some way and that others' evaluation of them is true, even when it is obviously false.

Example

Liam, nearly five, a bright, smiling lad from a supportive home, was one child who didn't get to join in. After just a few sessions of trying to get to play, Liam was becoming noticeably less confident. Obviously he was taking the other children's assessment on board. 'They tell me I'm stupid,' said Liam, 'maybe I am.'

Hartup (1992) understands this sad state of affairs. She explains that 'children's relationships with others both reflect and shape their understanding of themselves and their capacity to form relationships.' And as peer assessments are becoming more and more important to the children at this age, any rejection is devastating indeed.

Why had Liam had such a difficult time? He had recently moved to the district and joined the nursery in the summer term when the favourite activity was playing outside on large apparatus. Groups of children had already formed and there was a strong sense of ownership. Looking at Liam himself, his only apparent problem was with his motor skills. He couldn't climb as fast or jump from the climbing frame like some of the other boys. Was this why the group wouldn't let him play? Was this enough to make the child miserable? It seemed so. And yet that same group ignored other children with similar difficulties, but these children were not trying to force entry into the dominant group as Liam was.

As a result, the group was hostile; they called Liam 'stupid', although they had no evidence to show he was anything of the kind. Perhaps they didn't have the descriptive language to say what they meant and used 'stupid' as a general descriptor, but whatever the reason, this kind of name calling was unacceptable. Interestingly the same children didn't do this to children who had learning difficulties and they were very protective of a child with Down's Syndrome. It seemed that they had learned to be kind to these others, yet they ganged up against this new boy.

What were the staff to do? Removing the climbing frame was too obvious, and besides, many of the other children were enjoying it. The staff were doubtful that any verbal intervention on their part, such as asking the group to let Liam play, would be successful and they were afraid that if they tried and it didn't work, Liam's rejection would become obvious to other children who hadn't been aware of his difficulty. Giving the child extra help so that he could learn to jump from the frame was another considered possibility, but the staff knew that Liam was not ready to attempt this as he had not developed the coordination to enable this to be a safe move. They were also afraid that giving him special attention might be resented and make his problem worse.

Eventually, Liam joined an indoors group at the puzzle table. By that time he was anxious to let these other children see that 'he could do it', so that he wouldn't be left out again, and as a result he was quite aggressive and took over the play. After a short time, the other children walked away. He had tried to emulate his heroes by behaving as *they* did, yet the strategy did not work. Planning ways to get to play seems to be too difficult for some children. This makes it essential that adults find ways to help.

The importance of being the same

Even in the early years, and parents say 'earlier and earlier', children want to be the same, hence the pleas for the same clothes and trainers, the same haircuts and toys. They instinctively feel that this will help them either to be one of the gang if they are extroverts, or to merge in and not be noticed, if that is what they prefer. They are right, because choosing friends at this age can depend on children's rather superficial judgements which cover concrete rather than abstract factors. This changes as children mature.

Some fascinating research, again informal unpublished work by Edinburgh students, asked children of different ages to describe their friends. Craig, aged six, volunteered to talk about Sam, a 'special friend'.

He's a big big fellow – huge really with big feet and he sometimes falls over and bangs into me. He has fair hair and usually is kind but not always, for we fall out. He has a rabbit and a dog and I wish I had one too. Sam stays in quite a wee house with a green door at the front . . . .

As you can see his comments were mainly about appearances – surface qualities rather than enduring factors. Gemma's account of her friend was quite different. Gemma was 11.

I'll tell you about Lynne. She's my very best friend. She gets us all organised. She's the captain of our netball team and she's really dependable at turning up and giving her best shot. The good thing is that if we lose she doesn't blame one person because we are a team. That helps if the shooters have a bad day. She's not very clever but she copes and doesn't mind too much. She giggles a lot and keeps us all cheery.

Gemma was much more concerned with attitudes and capabilities than was Craig and these reports were typical of the children's comments at each age.

In the early years, children choose friends from those that are like them; they have a strong sense of 'them' and 'us' and will jealously guard against intrusion. They have strong stereotypes of those who are 'not like me'. This is why ethnic minority children gravitate to their own kind at this age (Aboud and Doyle 1995). It is quite natural, the children are establishing the mores of their own culture. This solidarity is more evident with boys' groups especially when they are quite newly formed – perhaps the timing of Liam's desired entry played an important part in his being rejected. This 'wanting to be part of a group' can even cause clever children to deliberately underachieve in school, as 'being different' means being left out! It is not difficult to see where parents' goals and children's ways diverge!

Having the same interests

The difference in playing patterns becomes obvious in these first years at school. Children are now moving beyond the boundaries of the family to find friends so peers become very important. At age four or five, cooperative play develops with children playing together for some sustained time to 'make up wee plays' (David and Christopher), 'dig tunnels and build a by-pass' (Robbie and Jack), 'do a ballet dance' (Laura and Petra). At this age the activity the children prefer to do is very important. Bee (1999) tells us that, 'shared play interests continue to form the major basis of these early years' relationships.' And so, one way for adults to try helping children who don't get to play, is to find the kind of thing they really enjoy doing and then plan how this could be introduced into the nursery curriculum or how the child could join others who also like that kind of play.

This sounds straightforward, but of course the child who has caused all this concern may not want to join the children who are engrossed in his kind of activity. He may know exactly who he wants to join and be willing to risk rejection rather than settling for another group of children. Liam did this. Although the staff had talked with him and his parents to find his interests – and that was animals – and asked him to bring in his favourite book to share with a group of children who loved animals too, this didn't work because Liam still wanted to be a part of the dominant group in the class, i.e. the group he saw as having the popular children!

However, as this activity-based strategy very often *does* help, the planning involves

- finding the child's interests and preparing a new initiative based on that (this is so the child doesn't have the difficulty of breaking into an already established game), then

- setting up the appropriate resources, hoping that interested children will come to play or, if that fails, inviting a group of like-minded children to join in.

But why should some children's company be sought and others shunned?

The characteristics of popular and rejected children

Some of the characteristics which cause children to be left out are beyond their control which seems most unfair. Physically larger but slim children and better looking children, especially if they have sunny temperaments, tend to be the most popular. Perhaps being popular allows them to smile more? Certainly it is difficult for rejected children to smile; they are understandably sulky or aggressive or withdrawn – all factors which may mean the rejection is sustained. This is often the fate of obese children, as is name calling. These children are rejected and ridiculed and are often driven to seek comfort in eating more. Sadly, they sometimes have other negative qualities attributed to them as well – laziness and stupidity (Stunkard and Sobel 1995) even when there is no evidence to bear this out. Seeing this happen, 'fear of being fat' can cause even primary age children to diet.

Popular children are 'non-aggressive, they explain things, they take their playmates' views into consideration; they are able to regulate their expression of strong emotions' (Pettit *et al.* 1996). In other words they can read other people's reactions and adjust their own behaviour accordingly; they have a well-developed emotional intelligence and are consistently positive. However, rejected children are often disruptive; they spoil games by being over loud and boisterous or, in an attempt to show power, they themselves reject children who offer to play. Rejected children often see aggression as the way to solve their difficulties. This can be seen if they are involved in even a slight accident. They interpret any bump as 'meant', i.e. as a deliberate act against them, and they retaliate in a hostile way in return. This exacerbates the cycle of despair.

Another pattern which is not popular is coercive behaviour, i.e. when children use emotional expressions to gain what they want. Other children recognise this, and while they may applaud it in a popular child who uses it infrequently to gain an advantage for the group, they deride it in a less popular child who uses it to gain a personal advantage. If these children have been 'successful' at home, through building a coercive attachment pattern with their parents, who perhaps want to compensate the child for not having friends at school, then the children will try this behaviour at school and be confused and distressed when it does not work. The trouble is that rejected children often find that the only group which welcomes them is made up of other rejected children, and the role model they provide may not be helpful at all.

Table 6.1 Aggression in Childhood

Pre-school children	Vent their rage physically, Tantrums (hitting the floor) are common and the children are inconsolable for a short time.
Physical response 'immediate gratification'	They 'hit out' if thwarted and may show little remorse as empathy may not be developed.
Primary age children	Significant change to verbal aggression – name calling/bullying resulting in longer lasting hurts.

As the children's social group and verbal capacity changes, so does the means of venting feelings.

And so children can inadvertently build barriers to friendship, and the sadness is that not getting to play at four often means the same at eight and ten. But this need not persist. Children can change their ways once they are able to understand that others have needs, once they are aware of the perspectives of others and how their own behaviour impacts on their own chance of becoming an accepted member of the group. Some children, unhappily, find great difficulty in making this change.

Understanding other people's perceptions

The development of a theory of mind

At around two years of age, children begin to understand that other people have intentions and that their behaviour will mirror these, e.g. if a child looks longingly at a cake, the likelihood is that he will try to get it! By three this kind of understanding deepens – the children begin to develop theories, 'If that person believes this, he is likely to do this, or perhaps that.' They also start to realise that someone may still want something, even though he can't have it. The understanding, however, has not deepened to the extent that they realise that other people may act on beliefs that are incorrect.

At four or five, there are still aspects of other people's thinking to be grasped. The four-year-old understands 'I know that you know,' but does not appreciate that this process is reciprocal. Such understanding develops for most children around age five to seven. This is a critical stage in the development of genuine reciprocal friendship and shows that children are less egocentric than Piaget (1954) claimed.

If two children at different levels of understanding try to make friends, it is not difficult to see how misunderstandings, which are developmental rather than intentional, arise. Most preschool children can accurately read the facial expressions for 'happy' or 'sad' but hardly any can deal with 'proud' or 'guilty'. This is complex enough for children without specific difficulties, how much harder it is for those who have real problems in this perceptual area, e.g. children with autistic tendencies?

One piece of advice given to help these children, is to immerse them in social encounters so that they have plenty of opportunity to see different modes of interaction. Only children and self-sufficient children who are content to play alone or in a very small group are more likely to have difficulty with interpretation of emotions and subsequent actions, than children who have a wider social group (Lewis and Freeman 1996). The dilemma of artificially engineering sympathetic encounters against knowing that this is not reality, is a difficult one to resolve. Perhaps the answer is to take one stage at a time and above all to keep the interactions calm and stress free.

Differences in children which make it difficult for them to play

Children with dyspraxia are one group who often find it difficult to play. They have difficulty in planning what they wish to do in a 'this then that' sequence of events. Given that this is problematic, they are even less likely to be able to interpret someone else's plans and appreciate the emotions that they could engender. This makes sustaining friendships very difficult.

Children who can't do the movement skills which other children value, e.g. play football or ride a bike, also tend to get left out as their more able friends abandon them. This causes anxiety, even depression. Fine motor skills are important too. Children who can't use a knife and fork or pour juice without spilling, suffer more as they get older as these skills become an essential part of socialising. Very often these children don't understand what is wrong. 'There's another party and I'm not invited again. Why not, Mum?'

Children with ADHD have similar difficulties even although the cause is different. These children are extremely restless. This prevents concentration for themselves and causes disruption and annoyance to others. They have a deficit in the ability to inhibit behaviour; they must react to any stimulus. Their problem is much more severe than that of the 'normally' restless child who is often urged to sit still. When other children get angry at being disturbed, these children can't alter their behaviour to comply and resentment builds up. Sometimes naughty children will provoke them as a way of setting up a distraction in the class. Their high level of impulsivity and lack of ability to concentrate also means that they cannot participate in any sustained game.

It is not surprising to find that half of these children display excessive aggressiveness which compounds their difficulty in making friends. This combination may well lead to bullying and delinquency or to children who are miserable and withdrawn. Drugs such as Ritalin help some children to be calmer, but their long-term effects are not known, and our concern is raised by the vast number of children using the drug.

Some children take the content of conversations too literally; they don't see the joke or appreciate the innuendo. One boy explained, 'I see them all laugh, so I go "Ha Ha" too, but I don't know why!' Teasing can be especially hurtful for these children, who, unable to understand laughing at others, certainly won't be able to laugh at themselves, or realise that some comments are meant to be shrugged off, not to be taken to heart. This is the kind of situation which leads to bullying and acts against children being able to make friends. And how do adults begin to explain this to children?

Children with any learning difficulty often have related social problems which make matters worse. The trouble is that because they are individuals brought up in different environments there is no one recipe which will be guaranteed to help them all.

Mixed age classrooms

McClelland and Kinsey (1996) found that if children experiencing difficulties in making friends could be incorporated into classes with younger children, the problem was often eased. These younger children did not make the same social demands. Moreover, they respected the older ones simply because of their age, and there was a chance for a new, positive start.

Parenting styles

The family plays a vital role in the social development of their children. The key characteristics of families which have positive, helpful children are:

- warmth or nurturance;
- appropriately high expectations;
- honest interactions;
- consistent standards and rules.

Children reared in a warm, supportive atmosphere where parents work with their children and encourage their children to achieve realistic goals have a higher self-esteem. They take on new learning with confidence, sure of support and encouragement at home. Children who understand and agree with 'home rules' and know that they will stand, and that playing one parent off against the other will not be tolerated, become more competent and sure of themselves (Kurdek and Fine 1994) and also less aggressive. They also interact with their peers in a similar supportive way, taking time to listen to their problems, i.e. showing altruism just as they have received it. The form of parental control is important if these outcomes are to be achieved.

Children who have parents who consistently use physical punishment in turn have children who are more aggressive to others (Eron *et al.* 1991). When children have many aggressive models and when these people seem to gain from it, it is no wonder that the children bring these hard and unacceptable patterns of social interaction to school. It is also no wonder that meeting a totally new way of doing things serves to confuse. The importance of teachers and nursery nurses understanding where the children are coming from is essential if their behaviour is to be understood. Thereafter, these professionals have to judge how they may best be helped. It is difficult but extremely rewarding to succeed.

Bringing it all together

The early years, then, see tremendous changes in all aspects of children's development. They move from being totally dependent to becoming relatively independent and able to make their own way at school. They have developed the language to be understood, the emotional strategies to control their feelings; they have learned that others have goals and ambitions and that they must have a turn too. They have become sociocentric rather than egocentric and are anxious to make friends. And when things don't go their own way, they have learned to explain rather than explode! They have the movement abilities to cope with everyday tasks and the skill to run and jump.

But not all children develop in the same ways. Some are anxious to take every learning opportunity while others are reluctant and shy. Some children can't get to play while others are in constant demand. The effects from the children's environment are complex and pervasive. Schools must try to understand the implications of disabilities and compensate for any disadvantages so that the children have the best possible chance to realise their potential. These are not easy things to do.

As children from many different backgrounds come together into nursery or playgroup to sample education (in a more formal sense), they are entering a new world of different demands and complex 'rules'. They need time and space to understand and the security of knowing that they will be able to cope. The staff, too, have a myriad of demands based on decentring, i.e doing their best to understand each child's participation in the fascinating process that is learning.

Teachers must find the best ways for very young children to learn. What are these? Through hands-on experience, through enjoyment and challenge, through freedom to develop. This can all be achieved through play which is planned and structured to enhance each child's capacity to learn. Adults are there to support and nurture the children. Surely this is the most important thing for them to do, for it is to the children that the future belongs.

A Developmental Record

Child's name .... Sex

Male   Female

Age .... years .... months

This checklist is for one child who is causing you concern. Please record the child's usual level of competence rather than focusing on one unusual occurence. If, however the child's movement is erratic, making a general picture difficult or less than useful, please say that this is the case.

    Before looking more specifically at motor development, please say whether you would consider that this was the child's only area of difficulty or whether there are other problems too.

Please tick if appropriate and add any other area of concern.

	Yes	No
Does the child have		
(a) Poor sight	☐	☐
(b) Low hearing	☐	☐
(c) A physical disability	☐	☐
(d) Difficulty in understanding instructions	☐	☐
(e) Speech difficulties	☐	☐
(f) Body-build problems	☐	☐
(i) very overweight	☐	☐
(ii) fragile	☐	☐
(iii) little strength	☐	☐
And is the child		
(g) Very tense and unsure	☐	☐
(h) Aggressive	☐	☐
(i) Lethargic – hard to interest	☐	☐
(j) Lacking persistence	☐	☐
(k) Seeking attention all the time	☐	☐

Any other difficulty? Please note below

The checklist now asks you to tick one box for each competence then give a mark out of ten for 'general coping ability' in that field. The boxes are 'Yes, can do it'; 'Some difficulty' meaning that the child needs real effort to cope; 'Severe difficulty' meaning that the child does not cope and 'Regression' which means that the child's performance is getting worse.

NB: This is a movement observation record to help teachers compile Assessment Profiles for school use or for gaining access to specialist help. It is not a test to determine dyspraxia.

Gross motor skills

Can the child	Yes	Some difficulty	Severe difficulty	Regression	Please give details
(a) Stand still, balanced and in control?					
(b) Sit still retaining poise?					
(c) Walk smoothly and with good poise?					
(d) Turn corners efficiently?					
(e) Walk on tip-toe with control (count of 6)?					
(f) Jump (two feet off floor)?					
(g) Kick a stationary ball?					
(h) Catch a large soft ball when thrown sympathetically?					
(i) Roll sideways and recover to stand with a good sense of timing and balance?					
(j) Crawl?					

Give a mark out of 10 for coordination in gross motor skills ☐
Please give further details if appropriate.

Fine motor skills

Can the child

	Yes, can do it	Some difficulty	Severe difficulty	Regression	Please give details
(a) Use a pencil/paint brush with control?					
(b) Pick up and replace objects efficiently?					
(c) Use two hands together to thread beads, build lego or do jigsaws?					
(d) Draw a person with some detail or parts?					
(e) Dress in the correct order?					

Give a mark out of 10 for dexterity in fine motor skills ☐

Emotional skills

	Yes, can do it	Some difficulty	Severe difficulty	Regression	Please give details
(a) Apper confident in following the daily routine?					
(b) Constantly seek attention?					
(c) Disturb other children?					
(d) Sustain eye contact?					
(e) Cope in new situations?					
(f) Appear aggressive or defiant?					

Give a mark out of 10 for emotional behaviour ☐

Please give further information below if you feel this would be appropriate. This could concern the areas already mentioned or different topics.

Intellectual skills

Can the child

	Yes, can do it	Some difficulty	Severe difficulty	Regression	Please give details
(a) Talk readily to adults?					
Talk readily to children?					
(b) Articulate clearly?					
(c) Use a wide vocabulary?					
(d) Listen attentively?					
(e) Respond appropriately?					
(f) Follow a sequence of instructions?					
(g) Understand					
i. spatial concepts – over, under, through?					
ii. simple mathematical concepts – bigger, smaller?					

Give the child a mark out of 10 for Intellectual Competence ☐

Social skills

Can the child

	Yes, can do it	Some difficulty	Severe difficulty	Regression	Please give details
(a) Take turns with no fuss?					
(b) Interact easily with other children?					
(c) Take the lead in activities?					
(d) Participate in someone else's game?					

Give the child a mark out of 10 for social behaviour ☐

Bibliography

Aboud, F.E. and Doyle, A.B. (1995) 'The development of in-group pride in black Canadians', *Journal of Cross Cultural Psychology* 26: 243–54.

Ainsworth, M.D.S. (1972) 'Attachment and dependency: a comparison', in Gewirtz, J.L. (ed.) *Attachment and Dependency.* Washington, DC: V.H. Winston.

Bandura, A. (1992) 'Social cognitive theory', in Vasta, R. (ed.) *Six Theories of Child Development.* London: Jessica Kingsley.

Bates, J.E. (1989) 'Applications of temperament concepts', in Kohnstamm, G.A., Bates, J.E. and Pettit, G.S. (eds) *Temperament in Childhood.* Chichester: Wiley.

Bee, H. (1995) *The Developing Child,* 7th edn. New York: Harper Collins College Publishers.

Bee, H. (1998) *Lifespan Development,* 2nd edn. London: Longman.

Bee, H. (1999) *The Growing Child,* 2nd edn. London: Longman.

Bennett, N. *et al.* (1997) *Teaching through Play: Teachers' Thinking and Classroom Practice.* Buckingham: Open University Press.

Bigler, R.S. (1995) 'The role of classification skill in moderating environmental influences on children's gender stereotyping: a study of the functional use of gender in the classroom', *Child Development* 66: 1072–87.

Brody, N. (1992) *Intelligence,* 2nd edn. San Diego, CA: Academic Press.

Bruner, J.S. (1966) *The Process of Education.* Cambridge, MA: Harvard University Press.

Bryson, M. (2000) 'Talk with me'. Unpublished PhD Thesis: Edinburgh University.

Campbell, S.B. and Pierce, E.W. (1991) 'Non-compliant behaviour, overactivity and family stress and negative maternal control with preschool children', *Development and Psychopathology* 3: 175–90.

Capron, C. and Duyme, M. (1989) 'Assessment of effects of socio-economic states on IQ in a full cross-fostering study', *Nature* 340: 552–4.

Claxton, G. (1990) *Teaching to Learn: A Direction for Education.* London: Cassell.

Cohen, D. (1987) *The Development of Play.* New York: University Press.

Connolly, K. and Dalgleish, M. (1989) 'The emergence of a tool – using skill in infancy', *Developmental Psychology* 25: 894–912.

Crain-Thoreson, C. and Dale, P.S. (1995) *Language Delay: Parent vs Staff Storybook Reading as an Intervention for Language Delay.* Indianapolis, IN: Society for Research in Child Development.

Cummings, E.M., Hollenbeck, B., Iannot, R., Radke-Yarrow, M. and Zahn-Waxler, C. (1986) *Early Organisation of Altruism and Aggression: Developmental Patterns and Individual Differences.* Cambridge: Cambridge University Press.

Darwin, C. (1872) *The Expression of the Emotions in Man and Animals.* London: Murray.

Dighe A. and Kettles, G. (1996) 'Developmental dyspraxia: an overview', in Reid, G. (ed.) 'Dimensions of Dyslexia', Vol. 2. Edinburgh: Moray House Institute.

Donaldson, M. (1979) *Children's Minds.* Glasgow: Collins Fontana.

Dunn, J. and Kendrick, C. (1982) *Sibling Love, Envy and Understanding.* Cambridge, MA: Harvard University Press.

Dyspraxia Foundation (2000) *Praxis Makes Perfect.* Hitchin: The Dyspraxia Foundation.

Eisenberg, N. (1992) *The Caring Child.* Cambridge, MA: Harvard University Press.

Ekman, P. and Friesen, W.V. (1971) 'Constants across culture in the face and emotion', *Journal of Personality and Social Psychology* 17.

Eron, L.D., Huesman, L.R. and Zelli, A. (1991) 'The role of parental variables in the learning of aggression', in Pepler, D.J. *The Development and Treatment of Childhood Aggression.* Hillside, NJ: Erlbaum.

Fagot, B.I. and Pears, K.C. (1996) 'Changes in attachment during the third year: Consequences and predictions', *Development and Psychopathology* 8: 325–44.

Flavell, J.H. (1985) *Cognitive Development.* Englewood Cliffs, NJ: Prentice Hall.

Gallahue, D.L. and Ozmun J.C. (1995) *Understanding Motor Development,* 3rd edn. Madison, WI: Brown and Benchmark.

Gardner, H. (1983) *Frames of Mind: The Theory of Multiple Intelligences.* New York: Basic Books.

Gerschwind, N. and Galaburda, A.M. (1987) *Cerebral Lateralization: Biological Mechanisms, Associations and Pathology.* Cambridge, MA: Massachusetts Institute of Technology Press.

Gesell, A. (1925) *The Mental Growth of the Preschool Child.* New York: Macmillan.

Goodnough, F.L. (1931) *Anger in Young Children.* Minneapolis: University of Minnesota Press.

Harris, P. (1992) *Children and Emotion: The Development of Psychological Understanding.* Oxford: Blackwell.

Hartup, W.W. (1974) 'Aggression inc hildhood: developmental perspectives', *American Psychologist* 44: 120–26

Hartup, W.W. (1989) 'Social relationships and their developmental significance', *American Psychologist* 44: 120–26.

Hartup, W.W. (1992) 'Peer relations in early and middle childhood', in Van Hasselt, V.B. and Hersen, N. (eds) *Handbook of Social Development: A Lifespan Perspective.* New York: Plenum Press.

Heaslip, P. (1995) 'Making play work in the classroom', in Moyles, J. (ed.) *The Excellence of Play.* Buckingham: Open University Press.

Henderson, S.E. and Sugden, D.A. (1992) *Movement ABC – Movement Assessment Battery for Children.* Sidcup: Harcourt Brace Jovanovich.

Isaacs, S. (1933) *Social Development in Young Children.* London: Routledge.

Katz, P.A. and Ksansnak, K.R. (1994) 'Developmental aspects of gender role flexibility and traditionality in middle childhood and adolescence', *Developmental Psychology* 30: 272–82.

Klaus, H.M. and Kennel, J.H. (1976) *Maternal-infant Bonding.* St Louis, MI: Mosby

Kuczaj, S.A. (1981) 'Factors influencing children's hypothetical reference', *Journal of Child Language* 6.

Kurdek, L.A. and Fine, M.A. (1994) 'Family acceptance and family control as predictors of adjustment in young adolescents', *Child Development* 65: 1137–46.

Lally, M. (1991) *The Nursery Teacher in Action.* London: Paul Chapman.

Lerner, R.M. (1985) 'Maturational changes and psychosocial development: a dynamic interactional perspective', *Journal of Youth and Adolescence* 14.

Lewis C. and Freeman N.H. (1996) 'Social influences on false belief access', *Child Development* 67.

Long, J.V.F. and Valiant, G.E. (1984) 'Natural history of male psychological health: escape from the underclass', *American Journal of Psychiatry* 141.

Maccoby, E.E. (1990) *Social Development, Psychological Growth and the Parent-child Relationship.* New York: Harcourt Brace Janovich.

Macintyre, C. (2000) *Dyspraxia in the Early Years.* London: David Fulton Publishers.

Macintyre, C. and Arrowsmith, J. (1988) *The Assessment of Motor Patterns.* Edin Dunfermline College of Physical Education.

Martin, C.L. and Little, J.K. (1990) 'The relation of gender understnading to children's sex-typed preferences and gender stereotypes. *Child Development* 61.

McClelland, D. and Kinsey, S. (1996) 'Mixed age grouping helps children develop social skills and a sense of belonging', *The Magnet Newsletter,* **5**(1).

Meadows, S. and Cashdan, A. (1998) *Helping Children Learn: Contributions to a Cognitive Curriculum.* London: David Fulton Publishers.

Munn, P. (1994) 'The early development of literacy and numeracy', *European Early Childhood Education Research Journal,* **2**(1).

Myers B.J. (1987) 'Mother-infant bonding as a critical period', in Bornstein, M.H. (ed.) *Sensitive Periods in Development: Interdiscipliniary perspectives.* Hillsdale, NJ: Erlbaum.

Pettit, G.S. *et al.* (1996) 'Stability and change in peer rejected status: the role of child behaviour, parenting and family ecology', *Merrill-Palmer Quarterly* 42: 295–318.

Piaget, J. (1969) *The Psychology of the Child.* New York: Basic Books.

Piaget, J. (1977) *The Development of Thought: Equilibration of Cognitive Structures.* New York: Viking Press.

Piaget, J. and Inhelder, B. (1969) *The Psychology of the Child.* New York: Basic Books.

Pinker, S. (1994) *The Language Instinct.* Harmondsworth: Penguin Press.

Pollard, A. (1996) 'Values, understanding and power', in Pollard, A. (ed.) *Readings for Reflective Teaching in the Primary School.* London: Cassell.

Roberts, R (1995) *Self-esteem and Successful Early Learning.* London: Hodder and Stoughton.

Rogoff, B. (1990) *Apprenticeship in Thinking.* New York: Oxford University Press.

Rovee-Collier, C. (1986) 'The rise and fall of infant classical conditioning research: its promise for the study of early development', in Lipsitt, L.P. and Rovee-Collier, C. (eds) *Advances in Infancy Research,* Vol. 4. Norwood, NJ: Ablex.

Rubin, K.H. *et al.* (1983) 'Play', in Hetherington, E.M. (ed.) *Handbook of Child Psychology: Socialization, Personality and Social Development,* Vol. 4. New York: Wiley.

Scottish Consultative Council on the Curriculum (1998) *Promoting Learning: Assessing Children's Progress 3–5.*

Shaefer, E.J. (1989) 'Dimensions of mother-infant interaction: measurement stability and predictive validity', *Infant Behaviour and Development* 12: 379–93.

Snow, C. (1997) 'Cross-domain connections and social class differences: Two challenges to nonenvironmentalist views of language development'. Paper presented at the society for Research in Child Development. Washington.

Sternberg, R.J. (1985) *Beyond IQ: A Triarchic Theory of Human Intelligence.* New York: Cambridge University Press.

Stunkard, A.J. and Sobel, J. (1995) *Psychosocial Consequences of Obesity.* New York: Guilford Press.

Tanner, J.M. (1990) *Foetus into Man: Physical Growth from Conception to Maturity.* Cambridge, MA: Harvard University Press.

Taylor, M., *et al.* (1993) 'A developmental investigation of children's imaginary companions', *Developmental Psychology* 29: 276–85.

Thomson, S.K. (1975) 'Gender labels and early sex-role development', *Child Development* 46: 339–47.

Trevarthen, C. (1993) *Play for Tomorrow.* Edinburgh University Video Production.

Vygotsky, L.S. (1978) *Mind and Society.* Cambridge, MA: Harvard University Press.

Warnock, M. (1978) *Special Education Needs: Report of the Committee of Enquiry into the Education of Handicapped Children and Young People.*

Wells, G. (1986) *The Meaning Makers.* Portsmouth: Heinemann Educational Books.

Wood, D. (1992) *How Children Think and Learn.* London: Blackwell.

Wood, L. and Bennett, N. (1997) 'The rhetoric and reality of play: teachers' thinking and classroom practice', *Early Years: The Professional Association of Early Years Education* **2**: 22–32.

Index